The I Ching and Mankind

By the same author

The I Ching and You (1973)

The I Ching and Mankind

Diana ffarington Hook

Routledge & Kegan Paul
London and Boston

First published in 1975
by Routledge & Kegan Paul Ltd
Broadway House, 68–74 Carter Lane,
London EC4V 5EL and
9 Park Street,
Boston, Mass. 02108, USA
Set in Monotype Walbaum
and printed in Great Britain by
Western Printing Services Ltd, Bristol

ISBN 0 7100 8058 1 (c)
ISBN 0 7100 8059 X (p)

Dedicated to the memory of my mother
Catherine Margaret Bellairs

Contents

Diagrams

Acknowledgments

The author's thanks are due to Nan Huai-Chin (Professor of Philosophy of the Fu Jen University, Taiwan), Dr Wen-Kuan Chu, Yvonne Jasven, Iris Knight, Zelia Pennington and Peter Wright for their assistance.

Thanks are due to the following for permission to quote from their books:

Curtis Brown Ltd for the Dragon-horse design (diagram 5) from *The Sacred Classic of Permutations, Chinese Ghouls and Goblins* by G. Willoughby-Meade, published by Constable & Co.

W. A. Sherrill for the chart of mutating hexagrams (diagram 21) from *Heritage of Change*, published by the East-West Eclectic Society.

Health Science Press for the twenty-four hour clock (diagram 27) and some extracts from the text of *What is Acupuncture?* by Dr E. W. Stiefvater.

Harcourt Brace Jovanovich Inc. and Routledge & Kegan Paul for the diagram from *The Secret of the Golden Flower* (diagram 10) by R. Wilhelm and C. G. Jung (Cary F. Baynes translation).

Princeton University Press and Routledge & Kegan Paul for diagrams and extracts from the text of *The I Ching or Book of Changes* by R. Wilhelm (Cary F. Baynes translation).

Franz Jung, Zurich, for extracts from *The Interpretation of Visions IV* by C. G. Jung from the Notes of Mary Foote, from the magazine *Spring* (1963) published by Spring, Zurich.

The Curtiss Philosophic Book Co. for extracts from *The Key to the Universe* by F. Homer Curtiss.

Samuel Weiser Inc. for diagrams and extracts from *Jupiter: The Preserver* by Alan Leo.

Introduction

Due to an increasing interest being taken today in exploring the ramifications of the human mind and its thinking processes, and the possible effects these may have upon Man's physical health and environment, a growing demand has been created for practical instructive works on the subject. For this reason I have undertaken a further investigation into the fascinating study of the *I Ching*, and produced the present work which may be regarded as an extension and elaboration of the principles of yang and yin as laid down in my first volume, *The I Ching and You.*

The *I Ching* cannot be dismissed merely as an ancient book full of incomprehensible symbols and magic spells, for had this been so, it is hardly likely that so great a thinker as Confucius would have spent all the time he did over it, and nor would the late C. G. Jung also have written so much on the subject. In fact, I do not think that any serious study of the *I Ching* can be undertaken without following in the footsteps of these two great scholars.

Let us begin by studying Jung's statement that because the principles embodied in the *I Ching** are engraved upon the collective unconscious† of the human race, it contains

* These principles are the pairs of opposites, that is, yang and yin in all their forms such as positive and negative, good and evil, father and mother, etc.

† A term widely used and understood by psychologists. The meaning of the word in its present context is thought to be sufficiently obvious to the layman. As this is not a dissertation on psychology, the

'magical' qualities of its own, and can therefore be used for psychic or divination purposes,* the symbols of the trigrams and hexagrams being the means by which its message is conveyed.

It seems that, because the all-embracing unconscious† knows, contains and takes into account everything, past, present and future alike, it is able to guide the unknowing separated conscious mind,‡ leading it, without error, to perfection and ultimate union with the Absolute Utmost, which the Chinese call T'ai Chi. The *I Ching* is not, of course, the only means by which guidance can be obtained. Meditation, prayer, dreams and astrology are some other avenues.

In order that a rapport may be established between the unconscious and the conscious, it is essential to recognize, and become familiar with, your own particular symbolic code; for although conforming to a basic pattern, as with physical features, fingerprints and so on, each person is nevertheless unique. This is why I stated in *The I Ching and You* (see p. 30) that, when using the *I Ching*, you must have a clear understanding with the unconscious as to exactly 'what you intend to mean what', in the same way in which people have to know and understand the spoken and written symbols of each other's language if they wish to communicate.

What is right for one person in certain circumstances may be quite wrong for another similarly placed as each has his own Tao, or path. A thing is only important to *you* if it has meaning specifically for *you*. Another person cannot be made to believe anything which he is not prepared to accept, however much you may attempt to make him do so, whether it be

* Many religious books or items can be said to be so endowed, for example the Bible which, it is recorded, was used for divination by St Francis of Assisi to assist him in a dilemma.

† See author's note on psychological terms, p. 1.

‡ See author's note on psychological terms, p. 1.

---

author feels that a full explanation of this term, which would be complex and involved, would be out of place and unnecessary here. If deemed necessary, the reader may follow up the matter by studying Jungian psychology.

faith in God, a particular religion, cult, idol, superstition, miracle, or merely whether or not another person is guilty concerning some purely mundane affair.

Jung speaks of a *synchronistic** principle governing so-called coincidences, everything being linked together in a moment of time, so that when the coins of the *I Ching* are thrown to obtain an oracle, the unconscious is activated and the pattern of that exact instant is revealed.

Therefore, there is a definite design into which everything fits with perfect harmony and synchronization within the cosmic whole, nothing being haphazard. Man *must* learn to attune himself to this pattern and its rhythm. In this respect life could perhaps be compared to a dance in which the steps to be taken are known only to the dancing master, who in this case represents the unconscious. Each dancer has to find out for himself what he is supposed to be doing and where he is meant to be at a given time, but, as only the dancing teacher knows the whole pattern, each is obliged to turn to him for instruction. Should the dancers choose to exercise their free will by ignoring him, they would undoubtedly blunder into and hurt one another in the process.

When mistakes are made in life, cosmic laws are instantaneously activated in order to correct them. These may take the form of cause and effect (Karma), reversal, compensation, balance and so on, all of which are illustrated by the patterns of the *I Ching* and referred to throughout this work. The balance of the universe has to be maintained regardless of the cost. If, during the process of alignment, tragedy or catastrophe strike, whether as the result of an individual's actions or a vast cataclysm of nature, it matters little, for, whatever the cause, the inexorable law must work itself out, though there is, of course, bound to be personal compensation where merited. The fault lies with the conscious circumstances which have been permitted to become out of harmony, and not with the unconscious itself whose law is perfect.

* See C. G. Jung's Foreword to the Wilhelm/Baynes translation of the *I Ching*, p. xxiv.

The unconscious speaks through omens and hunches received in the course of daily life, there being a significant reason why everything has its own particular shape, size or colour, why it moves in such a way, or is in its particular place at a given time; why an individual is situated in certain circumstances, and so on. But it is only when *you* take particular notice of these that they represent a symbol, immediately acquiring a far deeper significance for *you*, though not necessarily for anyone else.

'Heed the omens' the *I Ching* frequently admonishes, meaning by this that it is necessary to become aware that the unconscious surrounds and directs all the time.

Be this as it may, it is not very often possible to understand these omens because of interference from the reasoning mind and emotions. So when you are bewildered by a problem which must be solved, you will find the *I Ching* of inestimable value because of its symbolism. If, on the other hand, you prefer to do without the *I Ching* and wait until the conscious mind is asleep, becoming devoid of all its desires, problems of survival, occupation with self and material things, then a dream will convey the message, provided you are able to remember and interpret it correctly. A psychologist can sometimes help to point out its significance by finding out, through interrogation, what the various symbols dreamed about mean to you personally, so that the ideas of the psychologist are not projected upon your own symbolic code, thereby distorting it; your replies to his questions being given spontaneously so as to come from the depth of your unconscious* before having had time to be clouded by the thinking processes and reasoning power of the conscious mind.

The unconscious can be reached through any form of objective realization provided one stills the conscious mind, putting it to sleep, so to speak. At moments of quietude and serenity in meditation and prayer, the symbols of the unconscious will appear, and through your own subconscious, where they have to be sorted out and correctly interpreted, be

* See author's note on psychological terms, p. 1.

brought to the surface of the conscious mind. This is, of course, clairvoyance. It may take a long time of patient study to understand your own code. Constant practice will be necessary before you can attain the state of mind described by Shakespeare, where 'This our life . . . finds tongues in trees, books in the running brooks, sermons in stones and good in everything.'*

The general framework of a symbolic code is in the *I Ching*; all you have to do is put yourself into rapport with it, and then interpret the message its symbols have for you. In order to obtain the undistorted truth it is essential to use it in a quiet, reverent and objective manner, and moreover, once having sought its guidance, to follow this with faith and without question. The delicate connection forged with the unconscious must not, on any account, be abused or ignored because it can weaken in the same way that the voice of conscience may, until the link is no longer there. When this happens, man has only himself to blame if, as he calls desperately in the darkness for a helping hand, heaven appears to be unseeing and deaf to his cries.

The patterns of the *I Ching* reveal the manner in which the positive and negative cosmic forces balance one another as a giant pendulum swinging to and fro, now this way, now that, between the complementary pairs of opposites, the yang and the yin. All the myriad laws of the universe work in pairs. A few examples of the basic ones being as follows:

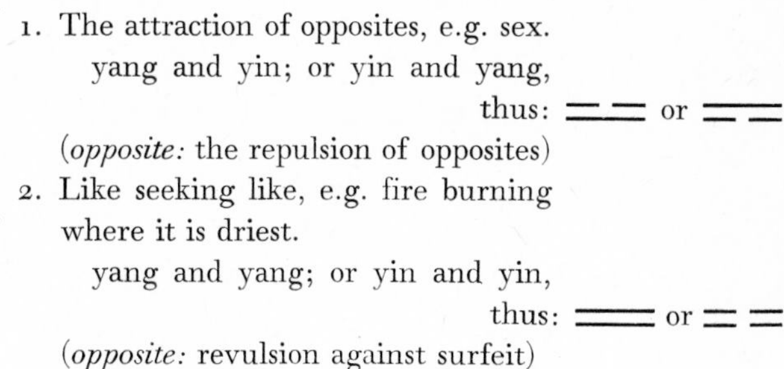

1. The attraction of opposites, e.g. sex.
   yang and yin; or yin and yang,
   thus: or
   (*opposite:* the repulsion of opposites)
2. Like seeking like, e.g. fire burning where it is driest.
   yang and yang; or yin and yin,
   thus: or
   (*opposite:* revulsion against surfeit)

* *As You Like It*, II.i.12.

3. The strong upholding the weak, e.g. the care of the young.
   yang under yin, thus: ☵☷
   (*opposite:* forces of good being held in check by the negative)
4. The weak following the strong, e.g. the pupil and his teacher.
   yin under yang, thus:
   (*opposite:* the strong suppressing the weak, the law of the jungle)

5. Taking the line of least resistance, e.g. the downward flow of water into a valley.
   yang and yin combined in trigrams, thus: ↓☵ Water
   (*opposite:* opposing, building-up, strengthening to overcome barriers) ☷ Earth
6. Growth and development through tension, e.g. pushing upward through the soil.
   yang and yin combined in trigrams, thus: ☷ soil (Earth)
   (*opposite:* accepting conditions and being swept along by the tide of events) ↑☴ wood (Wind)

When yang or yin is at the height of its powers, it overcomes itself and transforms itself into its own opposite. Jung calls this process *enantiodromia*,* a Greek word meaning a running in opposite directions or a return in an opposite direction when having reached a certain point.

To explain this further I quote from the notes compiled by Mary Foote out of the Seminar, *The Interpretation of*

* See the Seminar, *The Interpretation of Visions IV*, compiled by Mary Foote, published in *Spring* magazine.

Visions IV,* where Jung is reported as saying: 'If yin succeeds in swallowing and abolishing yang completely, then yang penetrates all the darkness and sets it on fire, and out comes the light again. Therefore if yin wants to overcome yang, or yang, yin; if a man wants to overcome a crowd or if a king wants to rule his people, he must be swallowed by the crowd, he must give himself over to them completely, because only thus can he appear in each one of them. That truth is symbolized in the Christian Communion. There Christ is supposed to be literally eaten; he penetrates the darkness of everybody and reappears in everybody.' In the Christian Communion there is a union of spirit and matter; of opposites, yang and yin. This 'conjunction' is one of the most difficult and important functions of the soul. The dreams of 'the great benefic', Jupiter, have to be brought down to earth and become manifested in the hard material world through the influence of Saturn, 'the great malefic'. The spiritual and material Man has to become integrated so that the body can express the soul. This is what Jesus did; and did he not say: 'For whosoever will save his life shall lose it'?† In other words, as I see it, in order to understand and love another person one must suspend any judgment or criticism of him, and then enter into his mind. Only thus, when one has absorbed his ideas as a person, will one be able to see life through his eyes. After this, there will be an interim period when you may almost seem to be that person because you have been concentrating on just him alone. However, far from losing your own individuality, you will instead have gained a dimension, for you will now know how he thinks and feels. Although you may not necessarily always agree with him, you will be able to get into discussion with him on his own basis. In this way you will give something of yourself to him, and at the same time, he will raise your consciousness. By joining with him,

* It should be borne in mind that these Seminars are not a manuscript of C. G. Jung, but notes written by students during, or even after, his lectures. So we can sometimes not be sure what he *really* said.

† St Luke's Gospel, 9:24.

you will be able to lead him, as Jesus did 'the publicans and sinners'.

The *I Ching* earns its second title, *The Book of Changes*, from the fact that its very core is concerned with the changing patterns of existence motivated by the unconscious and the power of thought. It can, in fact, be said to be a blue-print of the human mind by whose thoughts changes are wrought which ultimately mould the entire pattern of physical life.

The continuously evolving unconscious creates *archetypes*, as Jung calls them, and these in turn influence thought and physical manifestation in their various forms. The progression of the hexagrams of the *I Ching* are an example of how these archetypal patterns rise up from the depths of the unconscious and are born into conscious form. For those readers who are not familiar with *archetypes*, I will give an example which, though somewhat loose, will be simple to understand.

A generation or two ago when woman was expected to play the role of a wifely-cum-motherly person, her physical body was inclined to be somewhat plump and motherly. Today's woman, on the other hand, is considered to be a career-loving being, more of a playmate or companion to her man. Therefore she is now changing and emerging as a slim-hipped, flat-chested, boyish type of female. Thus the *I Ching* teaches that all intangible things, such as thought processes, magnetic forces and time, are the natural precursors of tangible physical existence and space. This spatio-temporal relationship to events is also contained in the philosophy of relativity, which, like the *I Ching*, embraces the hypothesis that what may be correct for one person in a certain set of circumstances at a particular moment may not necessarily be right for another similarly placed, or himself at a different time.

The heavenly yang line, of time and the mind, is undivided. It is the earthly yin line, of space and physical existence, which is separated.

The World is just entering the age of Aquarius which is a 'positive' Zodiac sign and stands for brotherhood, union and the pouring forth and sharing of knowledge with all mankind; unlike its predecessor Pisces, which is a 'negative' sign and the symbol of hidden things. When science and religion learn to combine instead of persecuting and decrying each other, great creative (yang) manifestations will be the inevitable result.

Man consists of body, mind and spirit, and therefore all three must be taken into account in his education, the ruling of his fellow men, the living of his daily life, in the diagnosis of trouble or illness and so on. For example, when the schoolteacher, ruler or medical man unite with the psychiatrist and the psychic, so-called miracles are bound to result. Mediums of the calibre of Joan of Arc and the prophets of old have existed down the ages, and do exist in today's world. They must be sought out and used. Only when there is a *trinity* in the headmaster's study, parliament, the consulting room and so on, will the *trinity* of Man be truly at-one with all life.

Man can learn through his unconscious how to avoid bringing suffering, either directly upon himself or upon his fellow man, with its cyclic, inevitable and therefore attendant repercussions upon himself. Your unconscious can help you to understand what is ahead, and teach you how to live wisely within the framework of your circumstances. The *I Ching* may be used as a bridge to this knowledge, for it will reveal the archetypal pattern of which you are a part. It is a guidebook to correct education and government, perfect health, superior happy living, universal peace and love.

1 | *Pre-heaven and later-heaven arrangements of the trigrams*

Those readers who have studied *The I Ching and You* will be aware already of the important difference between the two circular arrangements of the trigrams, and that these form the very basis of the *I Ching*. In this chapter I wish to enlarge upon them. They will be referred to throughout the book as either pre-heaven or later-heaven.

Pre-heaven (diagram 1) sometimes called:

Fû Hsî's trigrams
World of Thought
World of Ideas
Before the World
Primal
Sequence of earlier heaven

This is the primary arrangement of the trigrams in which opposite ideograms face one another across the circle. It is concerned with the balancing of complementary pairs of opposites, with the great cosmic forces of yang and yin, with time, thought, magnetic waves, the unseen, the unconscious, the unmanifested, the spiritual life, heaven, and with anything which is intangible. It illustrates that heaven's work with regard to the material world is that of maintaining a state of equilibrium between opposite forces.

The actual natural law of balance itself belongs to pre-heaven, because it is unseen; but when this is visibly manifested in matter, as a changing or changed state, it becomes the concern of the next trigram arrangement which is later-heaven. This arrangement deals with physical phenomena; the pre-heaven arrangement being behind and shining through later-heaven, as illustrated by the frontispiece arrangement of the two diagrams in *The I Ching and You*.

Later-heaven (diagram 2) sometimes called:

King Wên's trigrams
Inner World arrangement
World of Phenomena
World of the Senses
Sequence of later-heaven

This later arrangement of the trigrams, which follows the previous one, is primarily concerned with the variation of physical phenomena and tangible things. Tangible things which appear to rotate, as though through a circle, from a point in the east, where the trigram of the Arousing ☳ symbolizes their birth or beginning, round through all the other trigrams which in turn predict growth and harvest, and finally through to the position in the north-east where the last trigram, namely Stillness ☶, denotes their end or death (note that these particular two trigrams, that is, the symbols of birth and death, are opposites in pattern). Being sequential, this arrangement deals with changes wrought by the passage of time, such as the progression of the seasons; day and night; the birth, development and death of living things, of projects and anything else you wish to consider. It does not represent the passing of time itself, for, being invisible, time would be the concern of pre-heaven, but it deals rather with perceptible physical signs, such as the actual formation of a crystal, the ripening of fruit, the growth of a child and so forth. It refers to anything animate or inanimate, which, being of the earth, is impermanent and also in a constant state of change. Examples are place and space, a mountain, a building, a work of art, a piece of music, the physical body of Man as against his spiritual make-up, and all concepts which come into being, mature and eventually come to an end, die and decay. Death is the natural outcome of life; that is, its complement, not its opposite, for the opposite of life is stunted growth and distortion.

Later-heaven depicts the yang and yin force as being physically manifested as good and evil, strength and weakness, male and female, etc.

Pre-heaven's movement, as explained earlier, reacts across the circle from one side to the other, swinging to and fro from one trigram to its opposite, that is, from yang line to yin, yin to yang; from the trigram of the Creative to the Receptive and back again. The same back and forth movement takes place between each set of complementary pairs, for example:

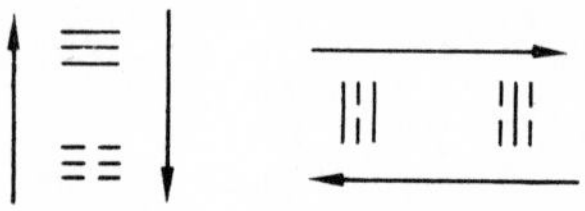

Whereas later-heaven's action is circular, thus:

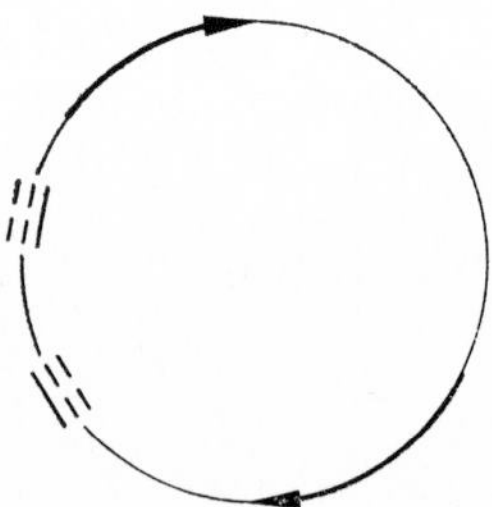

One has only to look at the manifestations of nature to see how many circles and curves there are. The sun, the earth, many fruits, the human head and even space itself are but a number of examples. Few, if any, absolutely straight lines or angles exist. Even when a twig or a rock splits, leaving jagged edges, these eventually become rounded off during the passage of time as the result of physical change. You have learned from the *I Ching* to heed the omens, and what better example could be found than this to illustrate that later-heaven, which relates to physical nature, is circular.*

Because pre-heaven, in other words, thought, time and the cosmic forces, is the forerunner of later-heaven, it moulds all action and manifestation in physical matter. How dynamic, therefore, is the power of thought! Pre-heaven is the sole means by which anything and everything can be diverted from its normal cyclic course in later-heaven. Thus one way in which miracles can be performed is through an alteration in timing, as the result of contact with heaven through prayer. However, magic and miracles can apparently only be performed upon physical matter within the framework of natural laws, very often through a speeding-up or slowing-down process of these.

The great Avatar, Jesus, performed many miracles, and it seems to me that when studying these, this pattern of altered timing becomes apparent in many of them. For example, when turning water into wine, he used the same element, merely speeding up the process whereby the rainwater was absorbed by the vine, eventually forming the fruit which was then gathered, pressed and fermented, all in a moment of time. The miracle of the feeding of the five thousand happened because the fishes were put back in time into a condition whereby they could propagate themselves, which process was then speeded up so that many generations were produced simultaneously. The bread was put back into a state where the yeast could expand the mass.

In the world of folklore, Cinderella was able to go to the ball as the result of magic. Incidentally, she represents the spiritual or higher Self, the Tao; whereas her two ugly sisters depict the lower, emotional and physical Self, aspects of yang and yin. In the transformation, the original elements were

* This, of course, must not be confused with the fact that in the *I Ching*, the yang, or spiritual symbol, is a circle; and the yin, or physical, is a square. For example, the Governing Ruler (yang) is shown by a circle ○, and the Constituting Ruler (yin), by a square □ (see *The I Ching and You*, pp. 59 and 60; and the text of the lines of the hexagrams in the Wilhelm/Baynes translation of the *I Ching*).

kept, only the timing being altered. Her rags evolved into silk; the white mice grew into domesticated horses; and the pumpkin, turning into wood, was able to be fashioned into a coach, all in a split second of time, at the flick of a magic wand.

With correct conditions, certain people can see into the future; this is because, as psychics, they are able to contact heaven where thought-forms, which precede events, take shape.

In the *I Ching* pre-heaven and later-heaven represent the difference between the spiritual and material life respectively. Spiritual things being united, eternal, unable to experience birth or death, beginning or end, are also symbolized by the unbroken yang line. Material things on the other hand, are symbolized by the divided yin line because they have a limited life-span and are subject to distance and death which separate; only a partial view of an event being seen at any one time and everything being capable of division.

Therefore the entire undivided pattern of any event, which must necessarily include its future outcome, is known only to heaven. Time which has not yet existed physically, that is the future, belongs only to the realms of spirit. On the other hand, the past (having already been lived) and the present have become a part of the earth, and can, therefore, be known by the physical mind as far as its limiting faculties will allow. Thus the future can only be known by contacting heaven or the World of Spirit.

However, it must be remembered that, because Man has free will regarding his thoughts as well as his actions, the patterns of the future can be changed to a certain extent, and for this reason fortune-telling can be a dangerously misleading practice, because of its possible inaccuracy. The *I Ching* must not be used for this purpose, as explained in *The I Ching and You* (see p. 11), because it is based upon behaviour patterns, and must, therefore, be consulted only for guidance. If, in the process of pointing the way, the *I Ching* happens to reveal future events, it is because it is necessary for you to know these for some reason, and also because it knows that such circumstances will definitely come about as the direct effect of the intervention of Fate, which, when occasion demands, will completely overrule Man's free will, or alter the entire pattern of the universe.

The reason why past incarnations cannot be remembered, which, after all, have already been lived, is that they have nothing to do with the present physical mind and memory, which, because it is of the earth, has become cut off or divided. If it should be desired to approach the Akashic records of these past lives, it can only be done through contact with heaven.

2 | *The tortoise diagram*

The tortoise (diagram 3) is extremely ancient, being said to form the very basis of the *I Ching*, upon which the sage, Fû Hsî, set out his pre-heaven trigrams through observing certain markings on the creature's shell. At first glance there may appear to be little, if any, connection between the arrangements of the tortoise and those of pre-heaven. However, the following figure shows that if the numbers of the tortoise diagram are placed in *numerical* order, the trigrams associated with them will then appear in the pre-heaven arrangement, provided that the Creative ☰ is switched from its present position in the north, to the south, as is customary with the *I Ching*; and that the Wind ☴ is transferred from the centre of the tortoise diagram to the new position in the south-west in Fû Hsí's arrangement (see facing page).

No trigram is associated with the number nine because it depicts non-change, which is explained later (see p. 59); and as the trigrams represent not so much objects as states of change, none of them, as such, can be connected with the number nine. On the other hand, the number five is the number of change itself (see p. 32) and is represented by the trigram of the Wind ☴, which moves from the central point, where yang/yin change takes place, to the south-west, which is the point of commencement of the interaction caused by it (see p. 18).

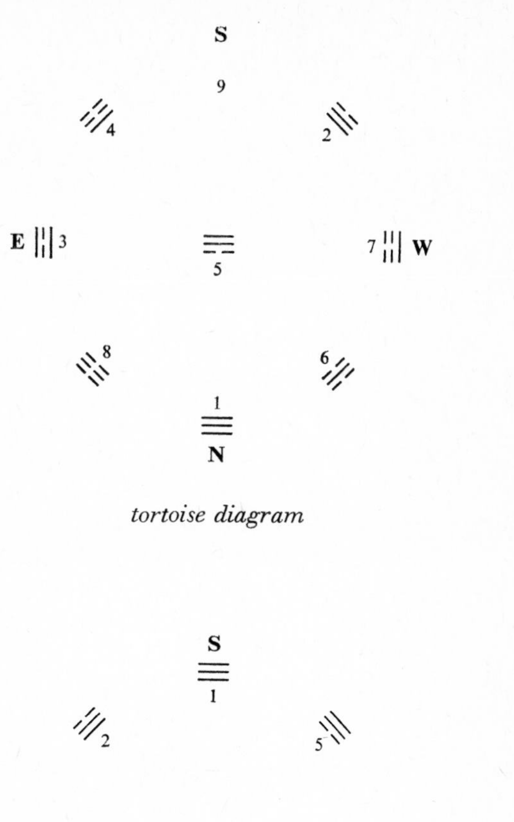

tortoise diagram

S
1
2
5
E 3
6 W
4
7
8
N

Fû Hsî's pre-heaven arrangement

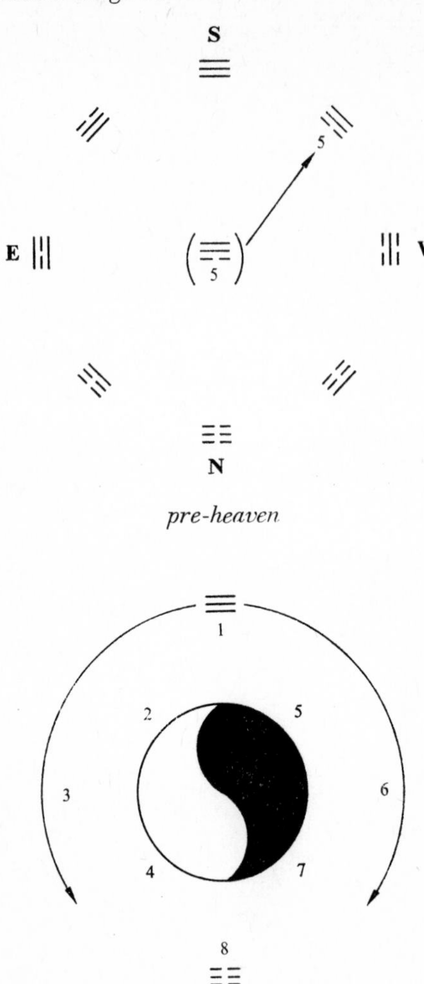

pre-heaven

the symbol of the I Ching

According to legend, the tortoise is said to have originally emerged from the River Lo. Diagram 4 shows that the River Lo Map, hereafter referred to simply as River Lo, has an identical number sequence with the tortoise, as follows:

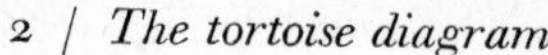

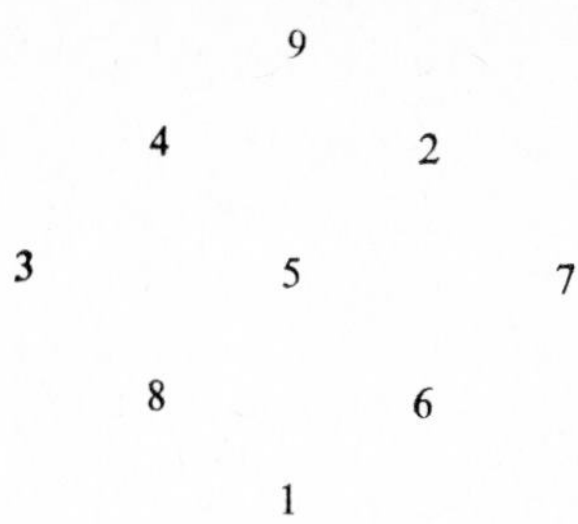

In addition to these numbers, the River Lo indicates the Five States of Change which will be explained in greater detail as the book progresses. The following figures show: 1. River Lo numbers and States of Change, and 2. the trigrams in the later-heaven arrangement with which 1. is identical, thus:

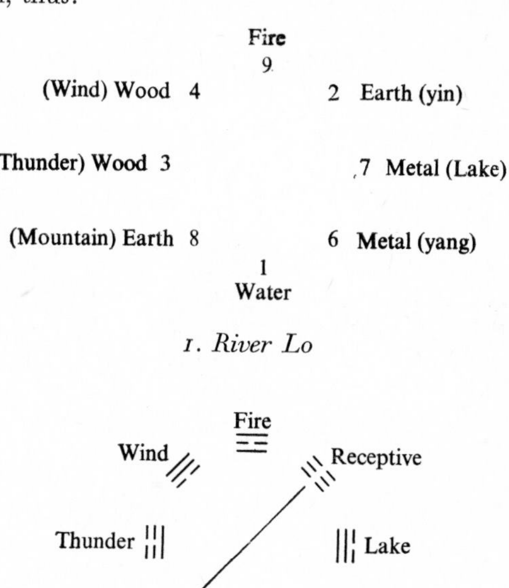

1. River Lo

2. later-heaven

In the States of Change of River Lo, the Earth is represented by two trigrams on either side of the diagram, the Earth being the only State of Change to be divided. The two trigrams are the Receptive (all divided lines), that is, the earth, yin ☷☷; and the Mountain ☶☶, which is composed mostly of earth. A line joining the two halves and passing through the centre, where change takes place, will slant as the earth's axis does (see p. 60).

In the tortoise, the number five at the centre divides it, so to speak, at the waist, that is east–west. This represents Man's solar plexus.

T'ai Chi, the Absolute Utmost or Primal Beginning, is said to be at the epi-centre of Shao Yung's circular arrangement of the hexagrams (see diagram 11, which is based upon pre-heaven, and therefore on the tortoise), being the exact point of balance between yang and yin in the north–south switch, as illustrated by the hexagrams on either side of this circle, where yang line is opposite to yin, and vice versa, around the entire figure. This will be dealt with more fully in chapters 6 and 8.

In his book, *What is Acupuncture?*, Dr E. W. Stiefvater states that the abdomen is thought to be the centre of energy of the physical body. It is certainly true that the umbilical cord is joined at this point; the continuous chain of this cord being carried on through the female who is, of course, yin. It is the life-line of physical bodies, which, being of the earth, are also yin; and it is through its separation (yin) that the creative (yang) force is born.

It was said by the ancient Chinese rulers who dwelt in the northern hemisphere, that if you want to conquer a city or armies, you must travel south in order to do so; in other words, you must attack from the north until you come to the equator, which is the waist or centre of the earth, then your direction must be reversed and you must travel north to attack. In the Second World War, Japan was victorious as she conquered southwards until she tried to cross the equator, and this mistake halted her. In China, the old emperors approached an army, or some place which they wished to conquer, by travelling to the north of it and then sweeping down to the south. (*Note:* these directions towards and away from the equator must, of course, be reversed in the southern hemisphere.)

In other words, the equator forms a dividing line, being the point of balance where day and night are of exactly equal length all the year round, i.e. half yang and half yin; and where the earth's temperature reaches its climax. This is symbolized by the merging of hexagrams 63 and 64 into one another, Fire ☲ being taken to represent heat; and Water ☵, cold, thus:

hexagram 63 { ☵ cold
☲ heat

equator (point of change)

hexagram 64 { ☲ heat
☵ cold

If one were to remain within hexagram 63, one would merely move up and down the lines within it, creating a reflection, as it were, of the same conditions. This mirror-like way of considering any hexagram, contains deep occult truth which is explained in greater detail as the book progresses. It is a paradox difficult to comprehend. By crossing the equator, that is, by mutating from hexagram 63 into hexagram 64, a state of transition is entered, which is the meaning of this hexagram.

Numerically, there are two reasons why the number five, found at the centre of the tortoise, is the number of change.

1. Five consists of two plus three. Two is the number of the earth, or yin; and three of heaven, or yang (see *The I Ching and You*, p. 16) representing the sides of the coins used for oracle-seeking.

2. Five converts yin (even) numbers into yang (odd) and vice versa (ibid., p. 67), as follows:

odd	even	even	odd
$1 + 5 = 6$		$2 + 5 = 7$	
$3 + 5 = 8$		$4 + 5 = 9$	

I should like to relate here the story of an encounter I had a short time ago with an African witchdoctor, because it has a direct bearing upon the link between the number symbolism of the *I Ching* and occultism.

The particular afternoon we met was hot and sultry, the setting picturesque. I came upon his hut in a clearing where groups of naked picanins, who had been playing in the dust, rose to stare wide-eyed with curiosity at my approach, whilst a few women in the background, their bodies draped with brightly coloured beads and little else, stood talking together apparently oblivious of me.

His house was the usual round mud hut, thatched with grass, and surrounded by a collection of similar dwellings. Entering the dark interior from the blinding sunlight outside, I was just able to make out the form of the great man who greeted me austerely, and, without rising, motioned me to sit upon an upturned tree-trunk next to him while he sat upon the mud floor.

As my eyes became accustomed to the gloom, I saw spread out before us on the ground, a conglomeration of bones, shells, sticks, stones, pieces of leather and other small objects. From amongst these he picked up and handed me three small sticks into which various markings had been burnt. Holding them in both hands, I blew upon them as instructed and returned them to the *sangoma*, who then began to 'throw the bones', as it is called locally, explaining as he did so that if the sticks fell one way up, it signified good luck, success or a man; and the other, bad luck, failure or a woman. This was, of course, just like the yang and yin of the *I Ching*. He threw, picked up and rethrew the 'bones' many times, and as he did so, called out numbers, explaining their significance. I was fascinated by the striking resemblance these bore to the meaning attached to the Tarot trumps, numerology and the *I Ching*.

He spoke very good, although at times somewhat broken, English, learned no doubt during schooling at some nearby mission where orthodox religious instruction had evidently neither failed to diminish his powers nor curbed his enthusiasm to use them. Listening enthralled to his dissertation upon the numbers, my eyes began to wander aimlessly over the heterogeneous collection of items laid out at our feet, when suddenly, in utter astonishment, I found myself staring at an empty tortoise-shell. Having obtained his permission to pick it up, I asked whether any particular number was associated with it; and on receiving the reply that all the numbers were, I then asked whether the tail concerned the number one, to which he nodded assent. Turning the shell around I pointed to its head, inquiring what number this represented. Although by this time I should not have been surprised, I was nevertheless startled when he stated that it was, in fact, the number nine.

How strange it is that a primitive African such as he should associate with a tortoise-shell the identical number symbolism of the *I Ching*, although he was separated from it by 5,000 years in time and from its country of origin, China, by many thousands of miles of ocean, impassable mountains, unknown languages and other barriers.

3 | *The dragon-horse*

In contrast with the pre-heaven tortoise which, because of its spirituality, is said to have been able to live on air, the dragon-horse shown in diagram 5, is a far heavier and more material creature, being associated with the later-heaven physical trigrams, which are supposed to have been revealed to King Wên by certain markings on the side of its body.

This fictitious creature is reputed to have emerged from the Yellow River breathing forth fire from its nostrils. The trigram of Fire ☲ in the upper position indicates that it was physically conscious, had intelligence and clung to heaven; whilst the trigram of the Water ☵ of the river at its feet symbolizes the instincts and the desire-nature or emotions of the physical body.*

The two trigrams depict the dual nature of Man, his spirit being a dragon, and his body a horse. The *I Ching* frequently uses a dragon to symbolize the creative power of heaven, and a horse for the physical vehicle; so that the dragon-horse represents the spiritual Man riding, with complete control, upon his lower physical nature. The symbols of the Egyptian sphynx and the Greek centaurs are analogous.

The configuration of Fire over Water is repeated in later-heaven, with which the dragon-horse is associated, where the trigram of Fire is placed in the south, above and opposite to

* See the meanings of the trigrams Fire and Water as given in *The I Ching and You*, appendix 3, pp. 106 and 109.

Water in the north. Fire and Water appear in this position both in River Lo (as trigrams) and the Yellow River Map (as States of Change).* Thus these four diagrams, the dragon-horse, later-heaven, River Lo and Yellow River are linked together in a physical sense through the material aspects of Fire and Water, only becoming connected with pre-heaven through the intangible number symbology of the heavenly tortoise, as will be explained more clearly in the next chapter.

The trigram of Fire stands for consciousness, the sun, heat, light, being analogous to the Christian concept of the Christ consciousness in Man, depicting selflessness and the higher nature, which is stressed by the fact that it occupies the top position in the dragon-horse. This trigram also represents the eyes which show appreciation of light and beauty; the heart, which is the centre of warmth and love; the intellect and mind which are situated in the head; all of which occupy the upper part of the physical body, forming the link with heaven above. Fire burns away from the earth, its natural direction being upward. The ideogram of this trigram demonstrates matter clinging to, and being enfolded within, the net of spirit, thus:

—— spirit
— — matter
—— spirit

On the other hand, the trigram of Water depicts spirit trapped within matter, thus:

— — matter
—— spirit
— — matter

Water, representing the desires and emotions, is unstable and confusing, reflecting or refracting the true image. This trigram also symbolizes the moon, which is a mere distortion or reflection of the true light of the sun, the very term lunatic

* States of Change have already been alluded to on p. 19, and will be explained fully in the next chapter.

implying one who is lacking in normal perception or intelligence, the antithesis to the meaning of Fire outlined above. As shown by the fact that it occupies the lower position in the dragon-horse, Water stands for the baser nature, selfishness, greed and lust. It represents the lower organs in Man's body; the sex organs which produce physical bodies; the stomach which feeds upon the earth; the kidneys and bladder which deal with water; the bowels which give off toxins and excreta which, in turn, fall to the ground. The natural direction of the flow of water is downwards towards the earth and darkness, away from heaven and the light. When comparing the trigrams of Fire and Water it should be borne in mind that they are not necessarily symbols of extremes of good or evil, for both have yang and yin lines in their symbol. Within every *I Ching* trigram there is both light and darkness, for even the great darkness of yin has its spark of light, shown in the yang/yin diagram as a tiny spot of white. However, broadly speaking, Fire and Water do represent such pairs as mind or body; higher or lower Self; unselfish or selfish; intuitive or instinctive; spirit or matter; and as such are the symbols of light or darkness, the latter being, of course, capable of reflecting light, having no light of its own, like a river or the moon.

This illustrates the theory held by many occultists that God descends into matter where consciousness is then born, a consciousness which is not only wakeful but has to become aware of itself as well, and what is perhaps more important, of things and more particularly people, in its surroundings.

In the houses of the *I Ching* it is stated that God's creatures perceive one another in The Clinging, that is in Fire ☲ (consciousness) (see page 86).

Jung says that the purpose of pain is to make Man aware of himself. Pain is represented by the trigram of Water ☵ (unawareness). It is caused by cruelty, selfishness, stupidity or lack of knowledge; the inability to alleviate it, by ignorance; all of which are facets of the absence of intelligence.

The mutation of hexagram 63 into 64 and back to hexagram 1 illustrates how Man has to raise himself from the lower state to the higher so as to return once more to heaven, and thus unite with the Divine from whence he originally sprang. This is explained more fully in chapter 5 which deals with the paradox of the reflected hexagrams of the *I Ching* and the mirrored triangles of the Kabbalah showing Man that everybody (and everything) is merely a reflection of himself, and that he is made in the image of God; and that the *I Ching* is, in fact, as mentioned earlier in the introduction to this book, a blue-print of the human mind.

Hexagram 64, which is the last in the series, depicts the trigram of Fire over Water, thus:

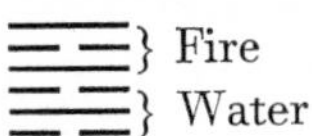

illustrating that it is the ultimate goal of Man to attain the state whereby the spiritual, unselfish nature is above and in complete control of the lower physical nature. He will then be in a state of transition, which is the meaning of this hexagram, ready to become creative and heavenly as in hexagram 1 ䷀, where the dragon of goodness flies across the sky, and all who see him benefit.* So the cycle of all the hexagrams begins again, each time on a higher spiral, which can be taken to indicate rebirth on earth, either as reincarnation, or orthodox Christian rebirth in Christ, or possibly as the death of the physical shell and birth into the celestial spheres, the *I Ching* teaching that there is never really any end, and where such may appear to be the case, it is merely a division and restarting point for something more creative and better.

It will be noted that though the trigrams of Fire and Water remain opposite one another in both pre-heaven and later-heaven, they do change position from east–west, to south–north respectively, as follows:

* See the meaning of hexagram 1 in the text of any translation of the *I Ching*.

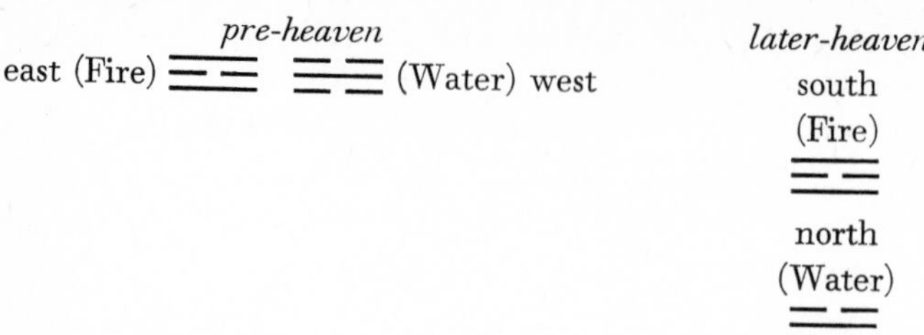

The outward omen of this is that Man, the intelligent, conscious ☲ creature, walks upright, whereas the animal, which is guided more by instinct ☵, walks on all fours. Taking these trigrams to represent Man's physical body, as already explained, he is shown either lying down with his head to the east, or standing upright. When at rest (east–west) because he is in pre-heaven, he is at-one with thought or spiritual existence. However, when standing up (south–north), he is in later-heaven and more in touch with physical existence.

If the trigrams of the Creative ☰ (positive) and the Receptive ☷ (negative) are introduced as the pre-heaven symbols of later-heaven Fire ☲ and Water ☵ respectively,* that is, if later-heaven is placed over pre-heaven so that the cosmic forces of the Creative ☰ shine through Man's mind ☲, and the Receptive ☷ through his physical body ☵, the link between Man and the cosmic forces can be seen, as follows:

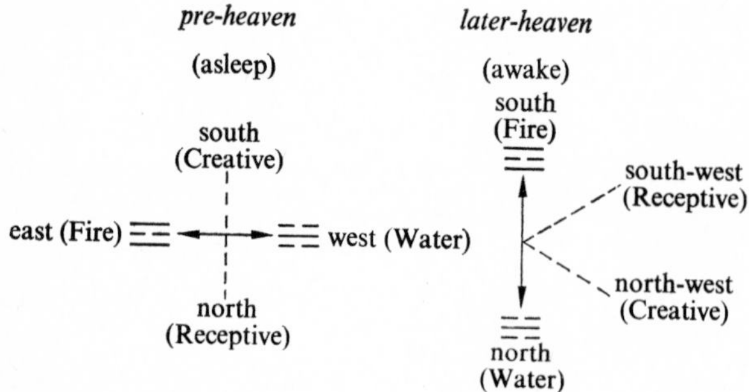

* See frontispiece diagram in *The I Ching and You.*

When Man is recumbent (east–west), that is, in a relaxed state, meditating, praying, possibly asleep or unconscious, he is within the pre-heaven World of Thought, where the positive and negative forces occupying south and north, are able to flow through him undistorted, putting him into a state of at-one-ment with T'ai Chi. Obviously therefore, the *I Ching* instructs that Man should sleep with his head to the east; the Christian churches are orientated thus, for the purpose of contact with spirit.

On the other hand, when Man is upright, awake and occupied with material wants, the struggle for survival and so on, he is within later-heaven where the positive and negative forces are no longer in the same rapport with him, making it more difficult for spirit to be contacted. However, he is never entirely cut off from heaven, being still able to make a link through the realms of thought, as shown by the above diagram, where the pre-heaven Creative and Receptive are behind Fire and Water.

The positions of the Creative and Receptive in the north-west and south-west (in later-heaven) and their links with pre-heaven can be explained astrologically (see p. 102).

By being the symbol of the eyes as well as of light and consciousness, the trigram of Fire indicates how various states of consciousness can be revealed by the response or otherwise of the human eye to light. For example, the eyes close in sleep, so open means day, light, consciousness ☲; and shut means night, dark, unconsciousness ☵. The position of the pupils of the eyes alters in sleep, unconsciousness and death, also when the mind is affected in fits, madness, etc. (Fire also being the trigram of intelligence). When dreaming is actually taking place, that is at the very moment when the higher self is directing or 'speaking', the eyes move rapidly. This is known technically as REM (Rapid Eye Movement).

Sleep is, therefore, the link through which mental balance with spirit and the cosmic forces is achieved, and without which Man would be unable to exist physically. Everything on earth must sleep at one time or another. During winter, which is a time of darkness, the plants rest and many animals hibernate. Every night ☵ (moon) the very earth itself turns away from the sun's ☲ invigorating power. Thus, whilst sunlight is demonstrated as being the instigator of developing intelligence and dawning consciousness in Man, sleep is also vitally important, for it is the time of recuperation and the period when spirit takes over to rejuvenate, improve and generally assist life to evolve; even so-called inanimate things being so affected because the Absolute Utmost (T'ai Chi) is within every atom. This link is the secret of psychometry, in which by holding an object in the hands and entering the realms of thought, it becomes possible to 'pick up' vibrations and learn of the object's history.

Perhaps the sleeping state is of far greater importance to Man than his normal waking moments. It is the time when he is linked with spirit and alive in timelessness, awake to the complete pattern and purpose of everything, the cosmic forces at this stage being able to flow through and revitalize him physically, whereas in his so-called 'awake' state he is out of touch with reality and the reason for life. Everything is distorted, reflected, veiled, muddled, misleading, divided, partially unknown and often seemingly purposeless. His knowledge of true facts is hampered and restricted, unless he is able to put himself into a completely relaxed state of mind through meditation and concentration, when, though possibly remaining conscious, he is able to contact the realm where all is known and purposeful.

From this it might appear that the semi-conscious existence of the contemplative monk or sage might be the correct way to live, but it is a suspended condition, not visibly creative. Jung points out that you cannot create by withdrawing into thin air.*

In the pattern of the Chinese cosmos (diagram 8), which will be dealt with later on, there are two basic triangles, one of which represents the spiritual life of Man, and the other its

* See Mary Foote, *The Interpretation of Visions IV* (notes on a Seminar by C. G. Jung), published in *Spring* magazine.

physical reflection upon earth, which suggests that Man has to be *in* the world, though not necessarily *of* it. He cannot dwell completely in the realms of spirit, ignoring the physical life altogether. To dope oneself with drugs, mesmerize oneself with pleasures or even spend the day in prayer, whilst ignoring the physical needs of those around, is not a possible way to live for any length of time because one cannot for ever escape the pull in the opposite direction. This pull will inevitably come as demonstrated by yang and yin. The life of pleasure will eventually pall. The hermit will ultimately feel the call to practical action. The only happy way is the road between the two extremes, that is, both through the earthly lower triangle of daily living and suffering, wherein Man must aspire beyond desire into the realms of spiritual existence, and through the upper triangle from which intelligence and light must reach downward to lift up the weary and ignorant.

This is the lesson of the triangles of the cosmos and the paradox of the invertible hexagrams.

The *I Ching* teaches the value of this middle path which it calls 'the golden mean', pointing out the need to avoid all extremes in behaviour in order to achieve a state of equilibrium between the cosmic positive and negative forces, from which Man can never wholly exclude himself. The Lord Gautama Buddha, it should be noted, taught his disciples to follow the 'noble middle path'.

4 | *The Writing from the River Lo, the Yellow River Map and the States of Change*

River Lo (diagram 4) and Yellow River (diagram 6) contain positive odd numbers shown as white dots, and negative even numbers shown as black ones.

The reason why odd numbers are positive and considered sacred, i.e. three representing the trinity, five the number of change, seven the perfect number and other odd numbers with their respective meanings, is because when an attempt is made to divide them into equal parts, the Monad, or the One (God) is left standing unaffected between the equalities, thus:

$$3 = 1 + 1 + 1;\ 5 = 2 + 1 + 2;\ 7 = 3 + 1 + 3$$

and so on throughout any odd number sequences, revealing the presence of spirit within matter.* The black and white dots form spirals which can be seen more clearly by consulting diagram 7. In the centre is the odd number five, positive, good, and therefore white. It is, of course, the number of change and controls the entire pattern entering the negative force and separating it into two halves, that is, dividing ten into two separate fives. This illustrates that though the positive five is capable of changing the negative force, i.e. splitting it asunder, it never changes its own nature, whereas the two negative fives, which represent the material existence, cannot

* See F. Homer Curtiss, *The Key to the Universe*, vol. 1, chapter 6, p. 61.

be further split and therefore have not the power of change within themselves, having had the intervention of the positive in order to bring them to their present state. That is, the yang or good force is undivided, yet can act upon and divide the yin; whilst the yin or evil force being capable of division cannot be creative on its own, which is illustrated by the symbols of the unbroken yang line and the broken yin, describing the difference between the nature of good and evil, the latter having no creative existence of its own.

In the middle of diagram 7 is a white vortex in whose centre T'ai Chi dwells. The negative black spiral around this, unable to live without the positive force, has to feed on the white, which it eventually consumes.

However, within this all-pervading darkness, there is a central spark of light which begins to develop at this very moment. For example, the dawn begins at midnight. Thus the darkness destroys itself, and the light begins to grow once again. This is the process of enantiodromia (see p. 6), and is illustrated by the *I Ching* symbol where within the darkness there is an 'eye' of light and within the light, darkness, thus:

Yellow River deals primarily with the senses and the physical manifestation of the States of Change (see *The I Ching and You*, p. 66) and, as has been pointed out, Earth is the only State of Change to be separated into two halves, each facing the other across the diagram. This black five plus five of Earth adds up to ten, which number appears only in Yellow River and not in River Lo. Ten is therefore the number of earth and later-heaven. In numerology, ten is the number of completion, there being, for example, ten Commandments and ten Sephiroth. Further explanations of this number are contained in chapter 13.

River Lo, which deals primarily with thought and spiritual existence, though containing the two opposite trigrams composing the Earth State of Change, which add up to ten, as outlined above (as do all the other States of Change in this map), is not concerned with Earth itself and the actual change caused. Each pair of numbers is divided into two digits, and the actual number ten does not appear in this diagram. The highest number of spirit and of pre-heaven is, therefore, nine. Nine is the number of non-change (see pp. 16 and 59) for heaven is unchangeable. Further explanations of this number are also contained in chapter 13.

To sum up, because five is the number of change, the earth can be divided by it into two separate fives (two being the number of yin) which when added together make ten. As ten, therefore, the earth is capable of being divided. When it is undivided it is complete, this is why ten is the number of completion. Heaven, on the other hand, is indivisible. If the central five white dots of Yellow River are set out in a row instead of in the form of a cross, the black and white dots form the following figure, which represents the trigram of Water, thus:

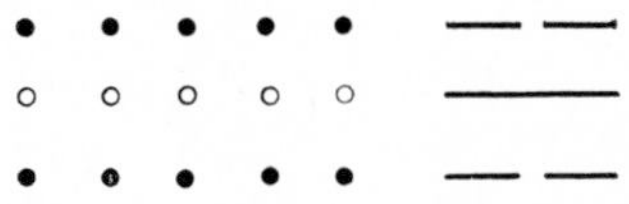

● ● ● ● ● — —
○ ○ ○ ○ ○ ———
● ● ● ● ● — —

As pointed out in *The I Ching and You*, Water is the first State of Change.

The above figure illustrates the sex act in which the Creative (white) enters the Receptive (black), and the female sex organ divides as the male enters (in-going), and subsequently again separates at the birth of the child (out-going), which is a further step in the act of creation. The entry of pollen into a plant and the later splitting apart of seed pods is a similar process. As the rain and the warmth of the sun, which come from the heavens, enter the earth, life is born. Thought and spirit mould material existence. The mathematical symbol for division ÷ is surely related.

Once a seed has entered the earth, or a baby is born, the first thing it requires is liquid, which in its original state is the rain. Thus Water is the first element which causes change, or to use the *I Ching* term, is the first State of Change. Besides being the trigram for Water, ☵ also represents the ears and, therefore, sound. It is said that the world was created by the sacred word *Aum*. When referring to Jesus, the Bible says 'In the beginning was the Word'.*

The second State of Change is Fire ☲, being the sunlight and warmth which, like the rain, reaches earth from the heavens, that is, the Creative enters the Receptive, and life on earth is begun.

The trigrams of Fire and Water are important because not only do they represent the conscious mind and instinctive nature respectively but, together with their pre-heaven counterparts, the Creative and the Receptive, they have ideograms differing from those of the other four trigrams, in that when inverted, they do not change their pattern, nor do they mutate into other trigrams, thus:

Water ↑☵ or ☵↓ Fire ↑☲ or ☲↓

Earth ↑☷ or ☷↓ Creative ↑☰ or ☰↓

On the other hand the other four trigrams change and mutate as follows:

Arousing ↑☳ becomes ☶↓ Mountain
Mountain ↑☶ becomes ☳↓ Arousing

Lake ↑☱ becomes ☴↓ Wind
Wind ↑☴ becomes ☱↓ Lake

* St John's Gospel, 1:1.

The States of Change of Fire and Water are unique because they operate on their own instead of in pairs, as do the other trigrams, that is, there is only one trigram for the State of Change of Fire, thus: ☲, and only one for Water, thus: ☵, as can be seen from River Lo.

The remaining six trigrams operate in pairs in the other States of Change and are as follows:

Wood comprises the trigram
Wind ☴ and Arousing ☳

Metal comprises the trigram
Creative ☰ and Lake ☱

Earth comprises the trigram
Receptive ☷ and Mountain ☶

From the foregoing it can be seen that there are two entirely different States of Change trigram arrangements, comprising Fire and Water on the one hand, and the remaining trigrams on the other.

Inner States of Change

Besides representing the intelligent mind and the instinctive nature, Fire and Water in the dragon-horse depict the higher and the lower Self,* and consequently these two specific States of Change deal with the make-up of Man himself, his physical body and mind and also his links with spirit, and therefore concern his spiritual, mental and physical evolution. In River Lo these two trigrams are found in positions south and north exactly and can therefore be said to form a central axis, as indeed do their pre-heaven counterparts, the Creative and Receptive. All four trigrams are also situated, one above the other, in the central pillar of the Chinese cosmos diagram (diagram 8), which will be referred to in detail in chapter 5.

* This repetition is thought necessary to stress the importance of the trigrams of Fire and Water as symbols of the conscious and unconscious.

These two trigrams, that is, Fire and Water, therefore depict the *Inner* States of Change.

Outer States of Change

The remaining three States of Change (making five in all) comprise the other six trigrams and deal with the realms outside Man and his relationship to them (see p. 55), and thus form the *Outer* States of Change.

The six trigrams which compose these three are manifest in such outward forms as the sky ☰, the soil ☷, the Wind ☴ (which also stands for Wood, that is, plant life), Thunder ☳, a Mountain ☶ and a Lake ☱. The latter four represent the four elements, air, fire, earth and water respectively, because they are *composed* of those elements; the lightning aspect of Thunder being fire. The first two trigrams are, of course, the positive and negative cosmic forces.

These trigrams appear around the edge, that is not across the centre of River Lo; and also on the two outer columns of the Chinese cosmos diagram.

The third State of Change is Wood, which comes immediately after Water and Fire. It is the first Outer State of Change after the Inner ones, and, as such, can be said to form a bridge between Outer and Inner States. It comprises the trigrams of Thunder (or the Arousing) ☳; and Wind (or Wood) ☴, both of which are symbols of dynamic change or movement because the trigram of the Arousing signifies quickening growth, and Wind, change; the latter, moving in the tortoise diagram from the *centre* to the *outer* point in the south-west, not only causes movement, but also in so doing becomes the agent which connects the Inner with the Outer States of Change.

The fourth and fifth States of Change, Metal and Earth, are relatively inert, yet, despite this, they contain within themselves the dynamic yang and yin respectively.

In the Metal State of Change, yang is coupled with the

Lake, the symbol of pleasure. Though composed of water it is more highly spiritualized than the trigram for Water because it contains two yang lines ☱ (Lake) instead of only one ☵ (Water). This fourth State of Change of Metal is highly masculine in form. In contrast, the fifth and last State of Change of Earth is truly feminine being composed of yin and the Mountain. The Mountain ☶, raised up from the Earth ☷ and composed of it, is closer to heaven and more spiritual than the earth, for it contains one yang line in its symbol.

Because change is relative to both time and space, it concerns speed, as the following figure shows. Here the six trigrams, omitting the Creative and Receptive, have been grouped in the first column, in pre-heaven which is concerned with time; yang and yin lines being opposite to one another.

speed of movement	*trigrams*	*State of Change*
Move on the earth at varying speeds. (Also symbols of rain and sunlight in the air.)	☵ Water ☲ Fire	combine to form the Inner States of Change of Fire and Water
Lie upon the earth and are motionless, but changing.	☱ Lake	combines with the Creative as Metal
	☶ Mountain	combines with the Receptive as Earth
Move in the sky at varying speeds. (Also symbols of wood and growth in the earth.)	☳ Thunder ☴ Wind	combine to form Wood

Besides their many other meanings, each of the trigrams relates to various members of a family. However, as pointed out on p. 55 of *The I Ching and You*, these vary in some cases according to whether reference is being made to pre-heaven or later-heaven, and are as follows:

	pre-heaven	*later-heaven*	
father	☰	☰	unchanged
mother	☷	☷	
eldest son	☳	☳	
eldest daughter	☴	☴	
middle son	☲	☵	changed
middle daughter	☵	☲	
youngest son	☱	☶	
youngest daughter	☶	☱	

(*Notes:* 1. The lowest line in pre-heaven indicates the sex.
2. The first four trigrams remain unchanged in either column, whereas the last four reverse sexes.)

The reason why the first four do not change sex is because they are the *causes* of change, in the same way that thought (pre-heaven) is the cause of change. The cosmic forces of positive (father) and negative (mother), continually switch from south to north and north to south. The Arousing (eldest son) and the Wind (eldest daughter) are dynamic forces of change as the reader already knows. For example, each parent normally produces a child which, if of the opposite sex, will inherit certain similar characteristics, that is, girls are to some extent like their father and boys resemble their mother. The eldest or first child is never normally a rhesus baby. However, it is capable of causing the second child to be rhesus.

With regard to the trigrams which do change sex, first notice the use of the word *middle* with reference to the second son and daughter, who have the same trigrams as the *Inner* States of Change which are in the *middle* of River Lo diagram. They are the later-heaven manifestation of pre-heaven's Creative and Receptive trigrams.

The trigrams of the youngest son and daughter each combine with either the Creative or Receptive trigrams to form the Outer States of Change of either Metal or Earth (see River Lo). The Creative and Receptive are the pre-heaven counterparts of Fire and Water respectively, as mentioned in connection with the middle sons and daughters who also change sex. All the offspring have a mixture of yang and yin lines within them, that is, they are a mixture of both parents, whereas the progenitors are either all yang (male, father) or all yin (female, mother).

It will be observed that the numbers allocated to each of the Five States of Change differ in River Lo and Yellow River diagrams. This is best explained by the use of the following figures:

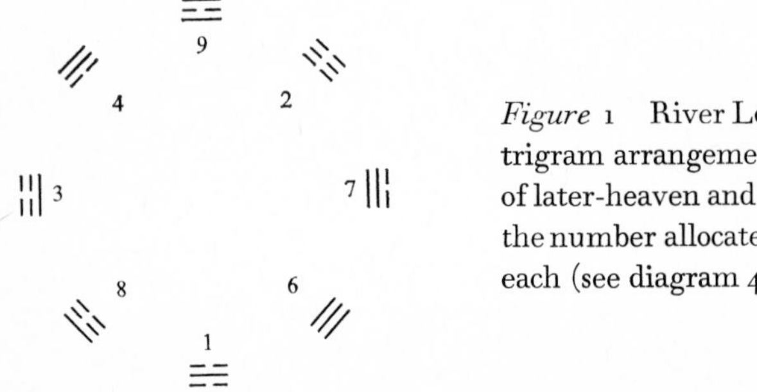

Figure 1 River Lo trigram arrangement of later-heaven and the number allocated to each (see diagram 4)

Figure 2 Numbers allocated to trigrams as above, but the trigrams have been placed in the position indicated by the numbers of Yellow River (see diagram 6)

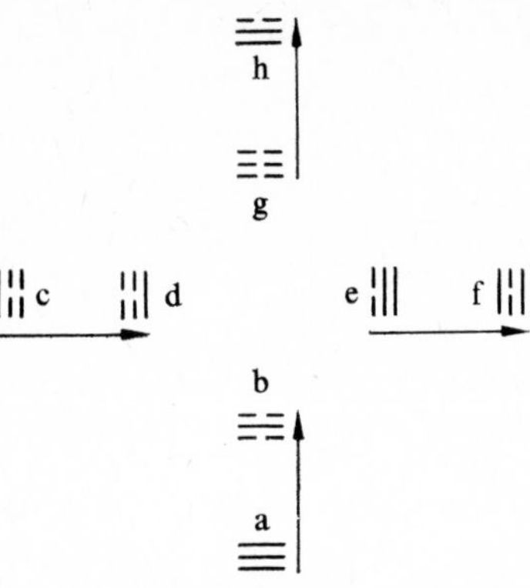

Figure 3 The trigram positions are identical with those in the above diagram, but the numbers have been replaced by letters, so that figure 4 can be more easily understood

(*Note:* the direction of the arrows shows the interaction of yang and yin, now outward-going, now inward, combining positive and negative together, but in alternating positions.)

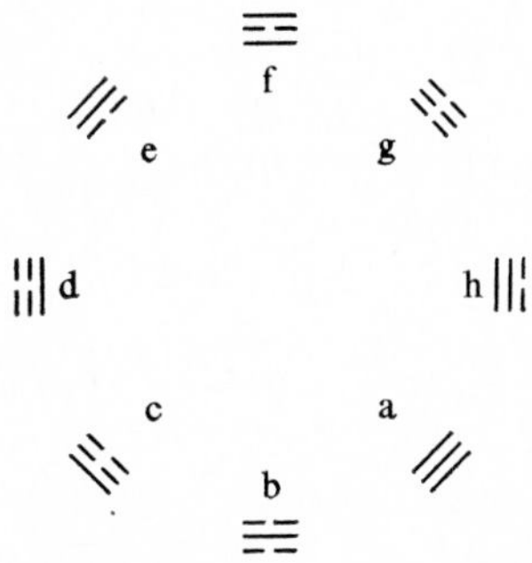

Figure 4 The letters indicate the sequence of the trigrams of later-heaven, and a return once more to River Lo

The following figure explains the link between the numbers of the tortoise diagram and the River Lo States of Change.

tortoise diagram numbers (concerns spirit)

River Lo States of Change with their trigram numbers (concerns material life)

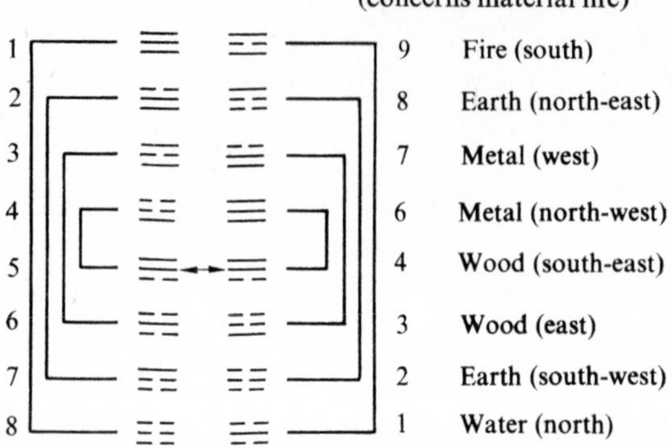

TORTOISE

(*Note:* opposite ideograms are linked together, therefore this column concerns pre-heaven.)

It will be remembered that in a previous chapter on the tortoise diagram it was explained that if the trigrams are placed in numerical order this would give the pre-heaven arrangement, which can perhaps be more clearly understood by looking at the above diagram, where the pairs of numbers total nine (the number of heaven and non-change), the number nine itself not appearing because this diagram concerns pre-heaven and thought which are the instruments of change. Therefore it contains instead the number five of change.

RIVER LO

(*Notes:* 1. Opposite compass points are linked together, i.e. north with south, east with west, etc.
2. Inner States of Change of Fire and Water are linked.
2. Outer State of Change of Earth trigrams are linked.
4. Outer States of Change of Metal or Wood are in pairs.)

The pairs of numbers in this column total ten, the number of the earth and, as five plus five, are capable of being changed. The number five itself does not appear because, as the diagram concerns later-heaven and physical existence which are incapable of changing on their own without the potent action of heaven and thought (pre-heaven), it contains instead the number nine (of non-change). The Wind (trigram of change) is the only trigram which remains in the same position in both columns. Occupying the central position in pre-heaven (left column) as the number five (central also in the tortoise which concerns pre-heaven), it moves across to the right column thus joining numbers four to six and forming a bridge, as it were, between pre-heaven and later-heaven.

Thus four and five (on the left) make nine (heaven); and six and four (on the right) total ten (earth). Nine is a positive, odd number, heavenly (pre-heaven) and yang; whilst ten is a negative, even number, earthly (later-heaven) and yin.

Furthermore, this link between the two columns joins the third State of Change (or first of the Outer States of Change), which is Wood, to the fourth which is Metal. Trigrams ☳ (4) and ☴ (5) on the left; or (3) and (4) on the right making Wood; and trigrams ☰ (6) and ☱ (7) on the right making Metal. The link between Water and Fire (as the first two (Inner) States of Change) with Wood (the third State of Change, and the first of the Outer States of Change) was explained on p. 37.

positive		*negative*		
1	and	6	produce Water in	north (first State of Change)
7		2	Fire	south (second State of Change)
3		8	Wood	east (third State of Change)
9		4	Metal	west (fourth State of Change)
5		10	Earth	centre (fifth State of Change)

The reversing action of yang and yin which produces the States of Change in Yellow River is shown in the table on p. 43.

(*Note:* Earth is the fifth State of Change and occupies the centre (see p. 94). Five is the number of change and occupies the centre of the tortoise. Change takes place in the centre of pre-heaven and at the equator of the earth (see pp. 18–20).)

The yang and yin force reverses back and forth in the above figure, as follows:

1(+) and 6(−)
2(−) and 7(+)
3(+) and 8(−)
4(−) and 9(+)
5(+) and 10(−)

10 divides returning once more to yang, Creative or 1(+) and so on.*

That is, by dividing into two halves, yin becomes productive (Creative) (see p. 34). Out of evil comes good.

As mentioned earlier, a clockwise direction is constructive, and an anti-clockwise one destructive, which is explained by the following table where the States of Change have been placed in the same circular sequence as Yellow River: Water, Wood, Fire, Earth and Metal.

Water produces	Wood	creative (clockwise)
Wood	Fire	
Fire	Earth	
Earth	Metal	
Metal	Water	

* 6 (−) and 2 (−) } illustrates like attracting like.
10 (−) and 1 (+) } illustrates the attraction of opposites.

Metal destroys Earth Earth puts out Fire Fire burns up Wood Wood (plants) absorbs Water Water rusts Metal	destructive (anti-clockwise)

This shows the importance of always moving in a clockwise direction when dealing with magnetism in any form, whether it be magic, alchemy, occultism, healing, the ritual of worship or life itself.

Besides the afore-mentioned directions, there is also an upward or downward movement, because good tends to rise and evil to sink, as has been explained by the dragon-horse trigrams of Fire (the spiritual Self) whose natural direction is to burn upwards; and Water (the lower Self) whose natural direction is to flow downwards. In addition to the above, the following are age-old symbols:

That which is open, and can therefore be seen by all, is positive because it is united, there being no separate sides, whilst a closed hidden thing is negative, because it separates the inside from the outside. In *The I Ching and You* (p. 69) an explanation was given about the closed squares of black dots and the open lines of white, of River Lo.

An upright cross + is positive, a diagonal one × is negative. Some of these occult truths are revealed if the positive numbers of River Lo are separated from the negative (see the figures on p. 46).

The numbers rise in sequence towards heaven, forming a cross, which is outward-going, symbolizing the figure of a man with outstretched arms in the act of welcoming or giving. It incorporates the four cardinal compass points together with the central point which controls change.

Besides the ancient Chinese scholars, the comparatively more modern Christians evidently understood the tremendous significance of the positive symbol of the cross with its transforming power for good, with its central number five (of change), from the limited Self, symbolized by the number one, into the limitless Self-less, shown by the non-changing number nine of initiation. This great occult truth with its magical power was hidden from the prying eyes of those who might misuse it, the real inner meaning being disguised in mystical language and revealed only to those who could understand and rightfully use its dynamic force.

positive, heavenly, odd, white numbers

south and place
of light (final initiation
into service to others,
brotherhood and selflessness)*
(the intuitive)

9

3 5 (change) 7

1
north
('I' am—the Self
and place of darkness)
(the instinctive)

direction of movement in the above figure

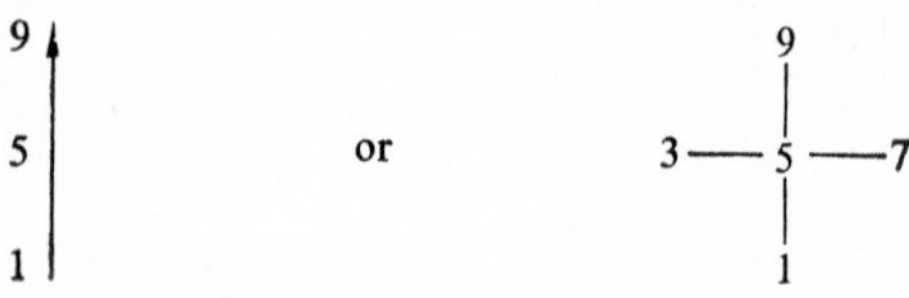

* A further explanation of number symbology is given in chapter 13.

The limitation of matter and material existence with its all-enclosing preoccupation with Self and the struggle for survival is shown in the following diagram:

negative, earthly, even, black numbers

4	2
8	6

direction of movement

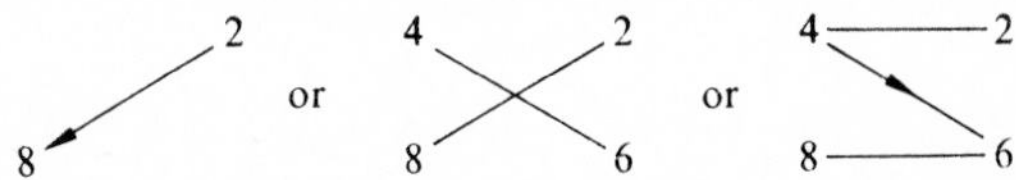

The numbers drop towards the earth, forming an enclosed limiting square and omitting any central focal point, and are thereby unable to change without the transforming power of heaven.

When added together, the opposite numbers in both of the crosses make ten which is the number of completion on earth, that is, the vertical cross of heaven will cancel out the diagonal cross of earth. This symbolizes the inner mystical truth of the forgiveness of sins by means of the cross, thus:

1 and 9 or 3 and 7 whose positive direction is $+$

4 and 6 or 2 and 8 whose negative direction is $\times$

How often the symbol $\times$ is used to indicate a mistake, to 'cross it out' as we say!

On the other hand, when placed together, the two crosses form

which is the Tarot magical eight-pointed Star of the Magi (or Venus) or 'l'étoile flamboyante' of the Masons.*

* See A. E. Waite, *The Key to the Tarot*, no. 17, the Star, p. 119.

Besides making a diagonal cross or square, the negative numbers can form a circle as the round shell of the tortoise symbolizes. Thus, by combining positive with negative the symbol of the cross within the circle appears which is the basic pattern of the sacred Mandala image, illustrations of some of which can be found in the last chapter of *The Secret of the Golden Flower*.

The potency of this symbol is well known to occultists and is used in the Christian Eucharist whose orthodox ritual is, not surprisingly, primarily concerned with the forgiveness of sins.

5 | *The Sephirothal tree of life of the Kabbalah, the Chinese cosmos diagram, the secret of the Golden Flower and the raising of the kundalini*

Diagram 8 shows the Chinese cosmos with its three columns and many triangles, the latter being three-sided figures which harmonize numerically with the three pillars. Two of the triangles are particularly important. This two and three symbolism represents the yin and yang, and as such is used in the coin method of divination (see *The I Ching and You*, p. 16), their total being five, the number of change. The diagram is explained as follows:

The triangles

All are reflections of one another. Of the two important ones, the topmost, which points downwards, represents the trinity of the Godhead, that is power (Father), wisdom (Mother or Holy Spirit) and love (Son), pouring itself forth upon mankind.

The lowest, with its apex towards heaven, represents the trinity of Man, that is spirit, mind and body, aspiring upwards so that he may become a true reflection of the upper triangle. When these two triangles become intertwined they form the six-pointed Star of David, or Solomon's Seal, thus:

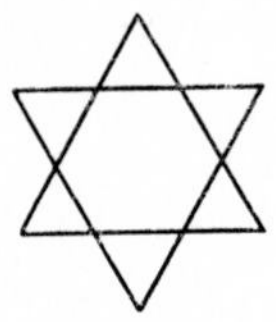

The central pillar

This represents Man, standing between the two triangles, learning to balance the positive and negative forces within himself, represented by yang and yin trigrams and the trigrams of the Inner States of Change, that is, Fire and Water. The symbol of Fire over Water in this column depicts hexagram 64 which, as the dragon-horse, represents Man's growing consciousness, his evolution and the raising of the fires of kundalini from the lower position in hexagram 63 } Fire to the topmost in hexagram 64 } Fire in other words, from the base of the spine to the head centre, referring to the controlling, by the conscious, of desires, instincts and unconscious actions. The yogi learns to subdue his involuntary body movements, such as breathing, heartbeats and circulation, all of which are unconscious, to the point where sometimes he can even simulate death. Only when the instinct of self-preservation is mastered, can a man bring himself to sacrifice his own life for another. The way to control the instinctive sexual drive is not by having intercourse repeatedly, whilst taking pills or having abortions to escape the consequences of such over-indulgence.

The path of evolution to the Creative, that is, hexagram 1, which is the symbol of total goodness or heaven, is, according to the *I Ching*, through the development of true consciousness; or, in other words, the attainment of complete control over the primitive instincts and desires as shown by hexagram 64 }conscious }instinctive, which, being the last hexagram, automatically joins up with the first because there is never any end.

The mineral and plant kingdoms of the earth are very beautiful, in many instances being near-perfect, but they are almost entirely physical, instinctive and, as yet, living in the unconscious ☵,* though there is, of course, the germ of consciousness within, in other words, the opposite pole, ☲.

Beauty is symbolized by the trigram of Fire ☲. The most attractive part of a tree or plant is its blossom at the top which is its sex organ. A plant is therefore symbolized by hexagram 64, thus:

☲ { flower
beauty, Fire (grows towards the light)

☵ { root
dark, heavy, Water (grows away from the light and towards water)

In Man, the sex organ has descended to the lowest portion of his body where it has become ruled by desire as symbolized by hexagram 63, thus:

☵ { desire, emotion

☲ { the subjugated
higher Self

Man must therefore learn to raise this force of consciousness back once more to the top position, that is, to the head centre or the same position as it occupied in the unconscious, unaware, unknowing or instinctive condition like the blossom of a plant. In fact, in occultism and certain religions this developed consciousness is actually spoken of as a flower, i.e. the 'Golden Flower' or the 'thousand-petalled lotus'. This process exemplifies the descent of God into matter and the ultimate union of Man with God.

hexagram 64	hexagram 63	hexagram 64
☲ God	☵ matter	☲ God
☵ matter	☲ God	☵ matter

* ☵ is the later-heaven manifestation of yin ☷ which is static; yang ☰ symbolizing movement (see p. 89). This is why plants do not walk about.

The symbol of Fire ☲ also refers to the eyes. When the third eye (situated in the middle of the forehead) is opened, that is when Man has become all-wise and all-seeing (truly conscious and clairvoyant), this symbol changes into the Creative (heaven), that is, the negative middle line of ☲ becomes positive ☰. Behind the later-heaven trigram ☲ is the pre-heaven trigram ☰. Thus the cycle begins again, with the Creative entering the Receptive.

The fact that all the nuclear hexagrams of any one hexagram eventually revert into either hexagram 1 or 2, or 63 and 64 reciprocating, was explained in chapter 11 of *The I Ching and You*, and illustrated in appendix 7 of that book. These four hexagrams are concerned with the Inner States of Change and the central column of the Chinese cosmos diagram. Their importance concerning the evolution of Man can perhaps now be more clearly understood.

In the garden of Eden (later-heaven), Adam ☰ and Eve ☷ saw ☲ (eyes, became conscious) that they were naked (primitive instinctive state ☵) because they had eaten of the fruit (later-heaven) of the tree (pre-heaven) of the knowledge ☲ (consciousness) of good ☰ (yang) and evil ☷ (yin).* 'Who told you that you were naked?' Adam was asked.† This is the parable of the awakening consciousness.

The positive and negative symbols within this central column of the tree of life can be compared to the intertwined serpents of Hermes' Caduceus. Mercury, as the Romans called him, was the messenger of the gods, his name being given by them to the fastest moving planet in our solar system. Astrologers associate Mercury with movement and also with the number five which, of course, is the number of change in the *I Ching*.

In this pillar heaven is at the top, with Fire‡ symbolizing

* The Creative ☰ and Receptive ☷ are the pre-heaven counterparts of Fire ☲ and Water ☵ respectively.

† See Genesis, 3:11.

‡ These two trigrams also refer to the sun ☲ and moon ☵ force in astrology.

the sun underneath, then below this the moon, and finally, at the lowest point, the earth.

In Yellow River, Fire and Water are separated by the central number five. Together with their pre-heaven counterparts, the Creative and Receptive respectively, Fire and Water combine in the cosmos diagram to form the plan of the centre of the solar system, but omitting Venus, as follows:

☰ heaven
☲ sun
5 mercury
☵ moon
☷ earth

In his book, *Worlds in Collision*, Immanuel Velikovsky may perhaps have been correct in assuming that Venus is out of place in our planetary system. However, I do not think that astrologers would go as far as he does in saying that Venus is an impostor in it; probably Venus is, as he suggests, an enormous meteor which collided with the earth. In her present position in the solar system Venus is on one side of the earth whilst Mars is on the other, these two planets being used, according to occultists (including astrologers), to provide the physical vehicles of male and female upon the earth. The astrological symbols Mars ♂ for male and Venus ♀ for female are often used in science.

It is possible that in the role of the foregoing, Venus may have been left out of the cosmos diagram, which after all is not really concerned with astronomy, because she could be represented, as could Mars, by the yang and yin symbols already there.

That some great meteor or planet did collide with the earth could well be true and could be responsible, as Velikovsky points out, for the day the sun stood still,* and for many other hitherto unaccountable events in the Bible which

* See Joshua, 10:13.

he also quotes; and for the fact that there is such a strange number of days in the year, very ancient sundials only catering for 360. The *I Ching* deals with circles divided into multiples of eight, and the geometric progression of two (yang and yin) has no affinity with 365¼. There are 360 degrees in a circle, and this number of days in a year would surely be much more in accordance with the mathematical exactness seen elsewhere in the patterns of the universe. Why then was this collision in space allowed to take place and not prevented by natural laws? Scientists believe that Pluto, although on the perimeter of our solar system, rightfully belongs because of its behaviour and make-up to the group of fast-moving planets nearest the sun, and would therefore also appear to be misplaced for some reason.

The previous figure of the arrangement of the trigrams representing the solar system illustrates how the sun came from heaven, the moon from the sun, and the earth from the moon, instead of the other way about, as is generally supposed. The occultists tell us that animals first lived upon the moon ☵,* later entering the waters ☵ of the earth, from whence, as instinctive creatures ☵, they have emerged, ultimately evolving into Man the conscious creature ☲.

The link between the moon and water, or flowing liquid, can be seen in the action of the tides, and the 28-day-cycle menstrual flow in women. The moon is also symbolic of a woman because, when waxing, it depicts the swelling of the pregnant womb, and when waning, the condition after the child's birth.

Man has, so to speak, first lived in water, not only as an animal on the moon, but also in the bag of waters within his mother's womb. At the present time, he is on the earth and will later evolve so as to exist in the air, he will then have grown wings and be able to fly, as do the angels who are superior beings. He is already trying his wings in the form of aeroplanes and space exploration. In millions of years' time,

* Water is the first State of Change.

when he will have adapted himself so as to be able to exist in the air, the earth will be as alien to him as water now is. Already a new archetype is beginning to form, as, looking for a new framework, Man is exploring the realms of the mind, leaving the earth by means of rockets, and even trying to lighten his body by slimming!

The age of Aquarius is dawning, and this is an airy sign.* By the time it has come round again several times more, Man should literally have become airborne. He must learn to fly back to the moon, then into the sun, that is, from the element of water, through earth and air, to fire; and then finally to go beyond the sun, to God himself.

The two outer columns

One of these is yang and the other yin. The left side of the human body is said to be yang and the right yin (see p. 106). These pillars contain the Outer States of Change trigrams, and are therefore different in nature from those of the central column, and deal more with Man's physical body and environment than with the forces which actually war within him. They can also be taken, however, to symbolize the empirical personality, in other words, that which of itself relates to the outside world (see p. 37).

The parts of the body referred to have been explained in *The I Ching and You* under each of the various trigrams. The columns also contain the four elements, whose unusual terminology as regards the trigrams has already been explained on p. 37.

This diagram of the Chinese cosmos should be compared with the Kabbalah (diagram 9), with which it has an identical symbolism. In both there are higher and lower triangles within which are, respectively, the trinity of power, wisdom and love (of God); and spirit, mind and body (of Man). Each of the words of the Kabbalah can be compared with the meanings of an *I Ching* trigram, as follows:

* Not, of course, the only Zodiac sign classified as Air.

Chokmah is masculine ☰, Wisdom (Creative).

Binah is feminine ☷, Understanding (Receptive).

Chesed representing mercy is linked with the trigram for the mouth and the joy-bringer, the Lake ☱.

Geburah meaning severity is the trigram for the feet, which have to be in constant contact with the hard earth; also the trigram for growth achieved as the result of tension and effort; the Arousing ☳.

Netzach is victory: the trigram representing the hands by means of which Man achieves; this trigram also symbolizes the serenity of the mountain which the candidate has climbed and upon which, as victor, he is elevated and may rest; the Mountain ☶.

Hod or splendour and power: the trigram of air, the breath of life, the creation of living matter upon earth; the Wind ☴.

Tiphereth and the trigram of Fire both represent beauty ☲ (the intuitional mind).

Yesod is the foundation. Sound, the sacred Word (see p. 35) is the basis of life. The ears are represented by the trigram of Water ☵, the instinctive mind and the beginning of everything because it is the first State of Change.

Malkuth is the kingdom which is associated with the number ten, as is the Earth ☷.

Kether is the crown, which being at the top of the diagram occupies the place of heaven; the Creative ☰.

If these two diagrams are compared with diagram 10, which illustrates the Chinese concept of the development of the Golden Flower,* a striking similarity will be found in all three. The light of heaven is reflected into the darkness of earth; positive and negative forces are at work, both within Man and his surroundings, which have to be balanced by him as he raises his consciousness to heaven. The raising of the Hindu kundalini fire is the same as the development of the Golden Flower of the Taoist, the blossoming of the thousand-

* Taken from Richard Wilhelm and C. G. Jung, *The Secret of the Golden Flower*, p. 74.

petalled lotus of the Buddhist, or the changing of hexagram 63 into 64 in the *I Ching*.

Numerically, the Kabbalah commences with the number one (God) at its crown, which descends to ten (the earth) at its base, from whence it rises upwards once again through the central column (the spine) to the head (representing heaven). In the Golden Flower diagram, reference is made to *Shên* and *Kuei* which are explained in the Wilhelm/Baynes translation of the *I Ching** as follows: *Shên* are the light spirits, outgoing and active, which can enter upon new incarnations; whilst *Kuei* are their opposite, that is, the dark spirits which withdraw, returning to their origin to assimilate the experiences of life just lived and completed. This represents the ebb and flow of life which perpetually expands and contracts.

* See p. 295.

6 | *Shao Yung's sequence (pre-heaven) and the numerical sequence of King Wên (later-heaven)*

The hexagrams of Shao Yung's circular sequence are shown in diagram 11, where the inner lines of the left half are all yang, and those on the right are all yin (cf. the outer columns of the cosmos diagram).

In diagram 12 this same series has been reduced to a circle of dots, each representing the position of a hexagram, the actual hexagram ideograms only being shown where these consist of the doubling of the trigrams, the latter being identical in position with the pre-heaven trigrams upon which Shao Yung's sequence is based (see *The I Ching and You*, p. 46). With the exception of those in the south and north, there are eight dots between each of the ideograms, which, together with any one ideogram (reading round the diagram), form a block of nine hexagrams. Taken six times around the circle this covers 54 hexagrams, i.e. $6 \times 9 = 54$.

South and north, that is, in the positions of the Creative and Receptive trigrams, i.e. yang and yin, there are only four dots between the ideograms, which, together with the ideogram of either the Creative or Receptive, form a block of five hexagrams. This completes the cycle.

$$\begin{aligned} 6 \times 9 &= 54 \\ 2 \times 5 &= \underline{10} \\ &\ 64 \text{ hexagrams} \end{aligned}$$

Nine, as the highest number of pre-heaven, is also the

number of non-change because, no matter to what number nine is added, the figure remains unaltered. For example, three plus nine makes twelve, twelve contains the integers one and two, which when added together, revert back to the original three; any number chosen, when added to nine, will so revert. Whilst nine is the number of non-change, five is the number of change.

From this diagram, the potency of five in relation to the changing yang and yin can be understood more clearly. This attraction and repulsion, swinging now this way, now that, is the ebb and flow of celestial magnetism which controls the balance of the universe.

Five spaces from the Receptive is the hexagram of Thunder or the Arousing ☳☳ which symbolizes the beginning of movement; whilst five spaces from the Creative is the hexagram of the Wind ☴☴ whose symbol is change. Thunder and Wind are complementary to one another in yang/yin line pattern and therefore opposite to one another in pre-heaven, that is, in Shao Yung's sequence. Together these two combine in River Lo to form the State of Change of Wood which represents organic growth. The five States of Change are physical manifestations; whilst the force which causes such changes is spiritual or thought-power, and so is pre-heaven, as is Shao Yung's sequence. The following figures will clarify:

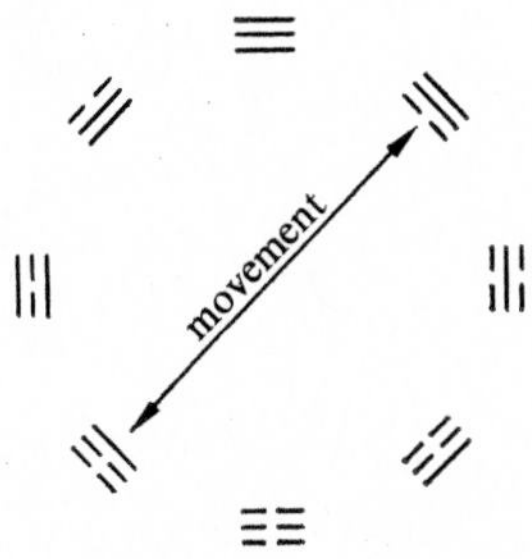

pre-heaven (thought)
Shao Yung's sequence

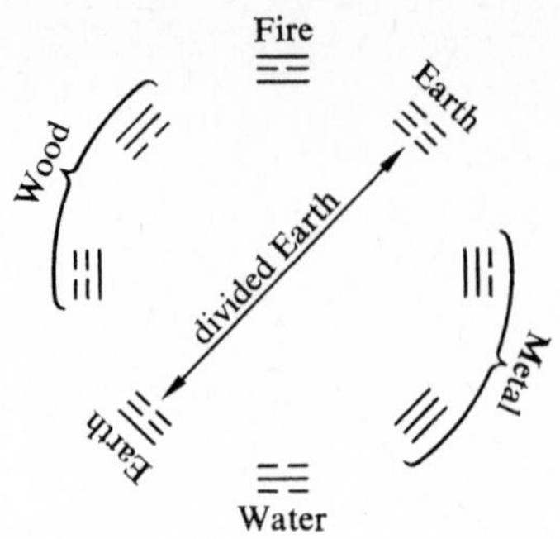

later-heaven (physical manifestation)
River Lo States of Change

Note in the above figures that the line of movement coincides with that of the divided Earth.

When Man has learned the signs which lead up to the point of climax where the cosmic forces are likely to change, thus altering the tide of events upon earth, he will be able to control or avert Fate to a certain extent. Already he is able to predict and locate weather conditions or cataclysms of nature caused by physical upheavals, and issue warnings to take any necessary precautions; but he is as yet unable to foresee these events earlier than the initial signs which have actually materialized, that is before the unseen, non-physical cosmic changes which cause them have started to operate.

These can only be known through contacting pre-heaven which is able to move backwards in time in order to reveal the pattern. This is what the *I Ching* means when it states that it has 'backward-moving numbers' (see p. 65).* 'Numbers' refers, of course, to the esoteric, pre-heaven tortoise numbers.

The bottom trigram of a hexagram represents the lowest aspect of it, and the top the highest; however, the *I Ching* refers to the lowest trigram as being the inner, and the highest the outer as follows:

* See the Wilhelm/Baynes translation of the *I Ching*, under *Shuo Kua*, discussion of the trigrams, chapter 2, p. 265.

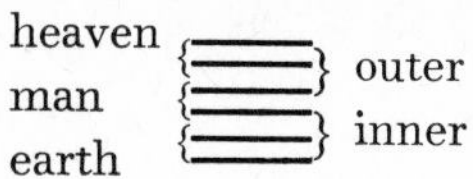

The top trigram with its association with heaven would be expected to be the highest (or inner) because it deals with the inner life. However, this can be explained by Shao Yung's circular sequence, where the hexagrams, being set out in a circle, show the lower hexagram on the inside, and the upper, outside (see *The I Ching and You*, p. 46). Nevertheless, this may still cause some confusion to the reader because, after all, the top trigram still does, in fact, represent heaven and therefore Man's spiritual nature, as the above figure shows.

This is a paradox of occultism which has already been touched upon as being contained in the reflected images of the Chinese cosmos and the Kabbalistic triangles. It can be further explained by the fact that because T'ai Chi is to be found at the very centre of Shao Yung's circle, the lowest line of a hexagram, besides being the most material and the nearest to the earth, is also the closest to God.

Each hexagram is, therefore, capable of being read either way up, as shown in diagram 13, that is, each contains within itself its own reflection.

In Shao Yung's sequence the individual lines of the hexagrams are also a reflection of each other across the circle, yang being opposite to yin, and yin, yang, for example:

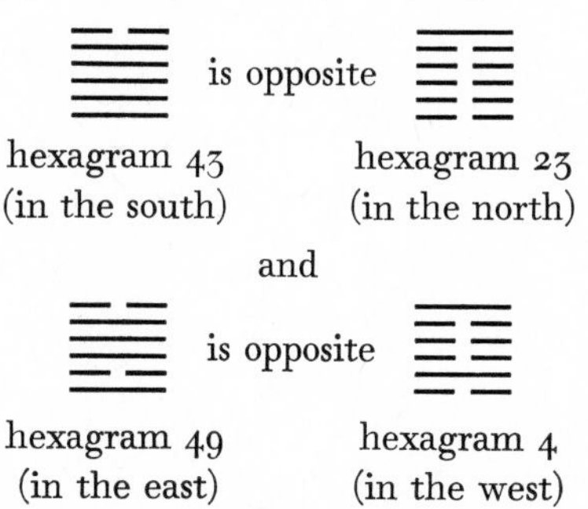

(See diagram 11—there are no exceptions.) This is based on

pre-heaven. However, King Wên's sequence of the hexagrams (see numerical order of the hexagrams in the text of the *I Ching*) relates to later-heaven (see diagram 13), where the patterns are placed in pairs of opposites, but not necessarily of yang and yin, that is, the entire ideogram is reversed. There are eight exceptions to this (i.e. four pairs) which are: hexagrams 1 and 2; 27 and 28; 29 and 30; and 61 and 62 (see diagram 13). In these particular pairs yang replaces yin and vice versa, it being impossible to obtain an inverted ideogram of them, because in trying to do so, it would only return to the same pattern each time, for example:

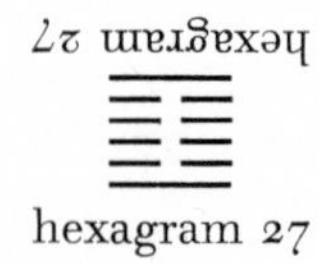

To sum up, not only does each and every hexagram contain within itself the positive and negative aspect of the situation it depicts, but it also has other hexagrams with which it can be associated, opposite in meaning, either as changing individual lines, which concern the pre-heaven sequence of Shao Yung, or as completely opposite ideograms, which concern the later-heaven numerical order of the hexagrams of King Wên. The hexagrams set out in circular sequence can be read in pairs of opposites across the circle, or from the outside inwards, or inside outwards, that is, the hexagram can be read either way up. Those of King Wên, however, can be taken in numerical pairs of which one hexagram is positive and the other negative,* that is, three is opposite four, five is opposite six, progressing in like fashion through the series (see diagram 13).

* Because odd numbers are positive, and even, negative.

7 | *The calendar hexagrams and more about the States of Change*

In diagram 14 the lines of the hexagrams in Shao Yung's circular sequence have been replaced by dots; white for yang and black for yin. Reading the entire circle from the inside outwards, that is, from the lowest line of the hexagrams to the topmost, the following pattern will emerge:

1st circle (innermost): 32 yang on the left, 32 yin on the right.

2nd circle: 32 yang at the top, 32 yin at the bottom.

3rd circle: 16 yang at the top, 16 yin at the bottom. Eight yang and eight yin opposite to eight yin and eight yang at the sides.

4th circle: eight yang at the top, eight yin at the bottom, the others being interspersed in blocks of four yang opposite four yin.

5th circle: four yang at the top, four yin at the bottom, the others being in blocks of two yang opposite two yin.

6th circle: two yang at the top, two yin at the bottom in the positions where the cosmic forces reverse; then yang and yin alternately around the circle.

This shows the build-up in a geometrical progression, illustrating the fact that the further Man goes away from the centre and T'ai Chi, the more he becomes tossed about from one extreme to the other by life's conditions.

Only twelve of the hexagram numbers have been indicated around the circle of this diagram. This has been done purposely in order to draw attention to them because they occupy salient points where the groups of black and white dots begin and end, that is, where yang changes to yin, and yin to yang. Reading anti-clockwise on the outermost circle, there are two white dots against hexagrams 44 and 1 combined, which change to black at the next hexagram, that is 43. The same type of change takes place in the north where hexagrams 24 and 2, which are black, change into white at hexagram 23. In the circle next to the outermost and still reading anti-clockwise, hexagram 34 changes the group of two black dots into white. A similar change from white to black takes place in the north at hexagram 20. In the third circle, reading inwards, hexagram 11 is placed at the last of the four black dots; and in the north hexagram 12 is at the last of the four white dots. In the fourth circle, hexagram 19 is the last of the eight black dots; and hexagram 33 of the eight white dots. In the fifth circle the thirty-two dots change at 19 and 33. In the sixth (innermost) circle black changes to white as hexagram 44 moves to hexagram 1; and white to black, from hexagram 24 to 2.

These twelve particular hexagrams have a variety of names such as special, sovereign, calendar, etc. They will be referred to throughout this book as calendar hexagrams, which, being placed at strategic positions around Shao Yung's circle, control the seasons. As this sequence refers to pre-heaven, this concerns time or cause, and not physical manifestations.

With the hexagrams set out as in diagram 15, a definite yang/yin pattern of light and dark is seen, indicating the brightness of the sun in summer and the lack of sunlight in wintertime, the yang lines increasing as the year progresses from springtime to summer, and then decreasing throughout the autumn with the coming of winter, coldness and darkness.

The *I Ching* is based upon the Zodiac and so the months of the calendar hexagrams refer to the seasons in the northern hemisphere; the periods of light and darkness have to be reversed for the southern hemisphere as explained in *The I Ching and You* (p. 26).

By comparing the hexagram patterns in diagram 15 with their positions in diagram 14, it will be seen that the calendar hexagrams move backwards, that is, anti-clockwise, in Shao Yung's sequence. In the Wilhelm/Baynes translation of the *I Ching*, these hexagrams are referred to as 'backward-moving numbers' because they are particularly helpful for divining and obtaining guidance about future action, in much the same way that it is possible, for example, to look 'backwards' at an acorn to assess the type of tree from which it came, and later, by moving forwards (in a clockwise constructive growth direction), to know the species into which it will ultimately develop.

In Shao Yung's sequence, with yang lines opposite yin and vice versa across the circle, May will be found opposite November, January opposite July, each pair throughout the year being six months apart. Thus the balance of nature is maintained; the time of the death of the year, that is its coldest point, being the very moment when the heat begins to return, and the life-force commences anew (an example of enantiodromia).

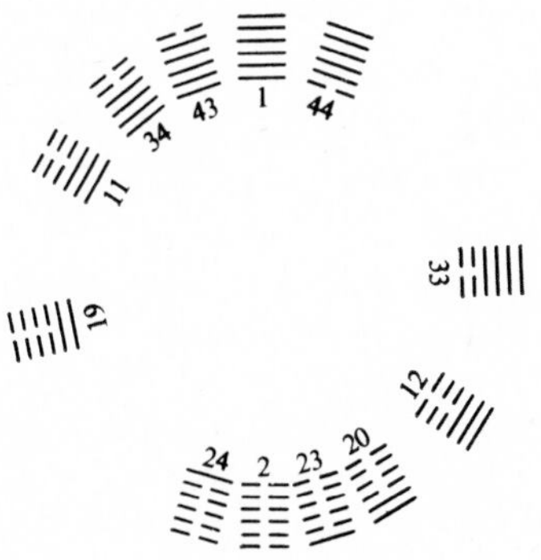

The calendar hexagrams placed in Shao Yung's sequence (pre-heaven, time)

1	2	44	33	12	20	23
1	2	43	34	11	19	24

The calendar hexagrams placed in King Wên's numerical sequence (later-heaven, place)

This latter pattern of opposites, because it is based upon later-heaven, will indicate the physical manifestation of the seasons, as against the dates when these take place, which are shown by the diagram on p. 65.

It will be observed that the calendar hexagrams contain all the trigrams with the exception of Fire and Water because the latter two concern the Inner States of Change and Man's evolution, and not the outer changing seasons. The other six trigrams which are present in the calendar hexagrams and so concern the seasons, represent cosmic forces of yang and yin together with the four elements having their different terminology (see p. 37) as shown in the cosmos diagram, and are as follows:

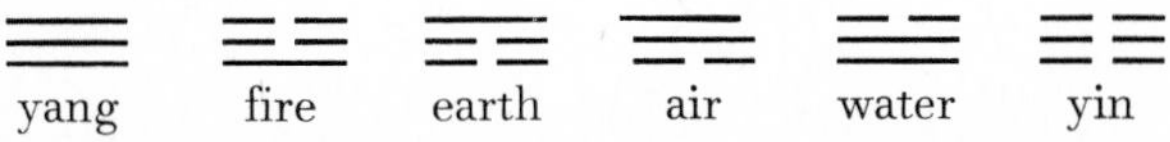

By forming a hexagram out of each pair of trigrams concerned with the Outer States of Change (see figure, p. 67), it is possible to begin to understand how King Wên attached the meanings he did to these, and from this beginning to proceed to an explanation of all the other hexagrams (in later-heaven).

As will be seen later on, these States of Change hexagrams also fit into Shao Yung's sequence as pre-heaven hexagrams.

The formation of these hexagrams is from the joining together of the two primary trigrams and does not include the nuclear ones (see *The I Ching and You*, chapter 7, for an explanation of the terms 'primary' and 'nuclear'), for otherwise the whole concept would become too complicated and the explanation of it too involved. There is, of course, nothing to prevent the reader from experimenting further with nuclear trigrams if so desired.

These hexagrams are grouped under their particular State of Change, as follows:

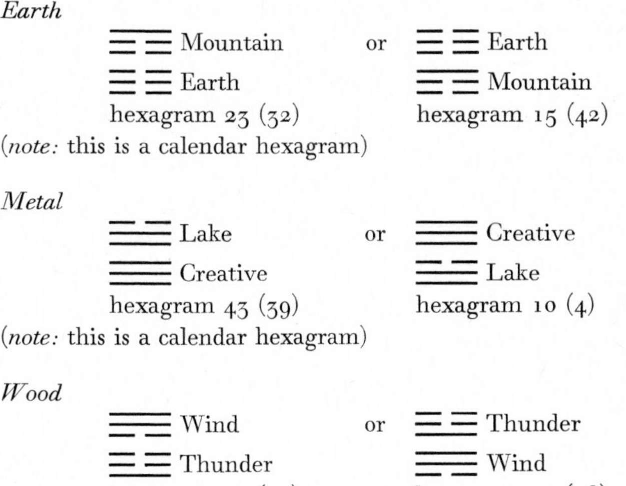

The hexagrams shown in brackets denote the pre-heaven counterpart (for an explanation see *The I Ching and You*, p. 52 and appendix 5).

It will be noted how the pre-heaven hexagrams (32) and (42) of Earth become the later-heaven hexagrams 42 and 32 in the State of Change of Wood. That is, the pre-heaven or thought hexagrams become manifested in later-heaven or matter. It will be noted that in so doing, their positions have crossed over, i.e. pre-heaven (32) has become later-heaven (42); and pre-heaven (42) has become later-heaven (32). This illustrates the bridge forged between pre-heaven (or spirit) with later-heaven (or matter), and how at the same time the earth or soil is able to mutate into plant life (Wood), such growth occurring as the result of a similar crossing-over process of forces hidden within the earth.

Earth State of Change

Hexagram 23 Splitting Apart

This hexagram occupies the position next to the Receptive (the yin, or earth) in Shao Yung's sequence. The Earth is the only State of Change which can be divided into two halves, hence this hexagram is the symbol of splitting apart. It is the calendar hexagram for the month of October when darkness and wintertime are ahead in the northern hemisphere. It is, therefore, the last stronghold of the yang (light) forces before they finally give way to yin (darkness). The text of the hexagram reads: 'Evil is not destructive to the good alone but inevitably destroys itself as well. For evil, which lives solely by negation, cannot continue to exist on its own strength alone' (see top line of hexagram 23, in the Wilhelm/Baynes translation of the *I Ching*).

This hexagram refers to the moment illustrated in Yellow River (diagram 6) when yin (10, the earth or evil) is split into two halves (5 and 5) by yang, thus:

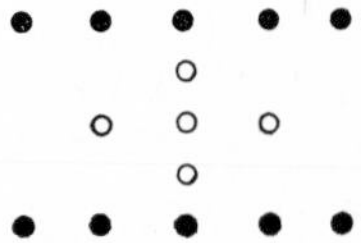

It is the moment of conception (see p. 34) when the male divides the female (yin) to enter her, then divides himself so that he may release the sperm for her to receive. Then yang collapses (see text of top line of hexagram 23). This also illustrates the splitting open of fruit in order to release the seed, and the subsequent splitting apart of the earth to receive it, when thereafter the fruit collapses and rots, or in other words, the fruit destroys itself. The image of this hexagram is of a Mountain over the Earth, or the Earth rising up to form a Mountain, thus: ☶} Mountain ☷} Earth. It is the symbol of the swelling of the fruit on a tree, or of a pregnant woman (the waxing moon) which will eventually split apart to release the seed or child, and thereby become reduced to its original size (the waning moon). Existing no longer, the Mountain becomes level once more, and forms hexagram 2, next to it in Shao Yung's sequence, which is the image of the Earth over the Earth, instead of a Mountain over the Earth. Hexagram 2 symbolizes a woman seeking the yang, or a mother for she has created a child (yang).

The pre-heaven hexagram of 23 is 32 whose title is Duration, which symbolizes continuity or the necessity to seek a mate and fertilize in order to lend endurance to the species. The connection between these two hexagrams is obvious.

Next to hexagram 23 ䷖ in King Wên's numerical sequence and its opposite in pattern is hexagram 24. ䷗

Although this is not one of the six hexagrams formed by the States of Change (see p. 67), it is nevertheless one of the calendar hexagrams. It is called Return, for instead of all the yin lines combining to push out the remaining yang line at the top, as in hexagram 23, here there is the reverse situation in which the strong yang line at the bottom represents the return of goodness and strength and right behaviour. In other words, the forces of light, having entered the hexagram from below, will be on the increase until the dark forces have been completely eliminated. Being the calendar hexagram for the month of December when the shortest day is reached, it depicts the exact moment when the days begin to lengthen. From this time onwards the yang force begins to build up, as shown by the increasing number of yang lines in the calendar hexagrams for the months ahead, until the climax of total yang is achieved.

The other Earth State of Change hexagram is 15, Modesty,

and although this is not one of the calendar hexagrams, it is considered of great importance, for humility is one of the prime virtues, particularly considered so by the Chinese. As the result of this, it is the only hexagram in which every one of the lines contained in it is favourable.

Its image is of the Earth over the Mountain, thus:

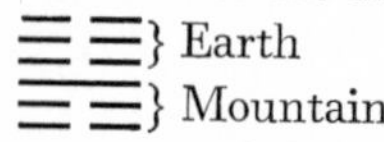

which is the natural outcome of the previous Earth Change hexagram 23, Splitting Apart, for it deals with the reduction in size of that which has become large, in the same way that humility or modesty is the reduction of oneself. Physically, after the sex act, the male organ is reduced in size; and the female organ, after her nine months' full cycle has been completed, resulting in the birth of her child, is also reduced.

It illustrates the natural law whereby in order to balance the universe, greatness in size leads ultimately to reduction, and smallness to increase. For example, a large or fully grown plant or person produces a tiny seed, which in turn grows big. Where the surface of the earth rises up, the rain will beat upon this mound, eventually washing it away. When an organ of the body is sufficiently full, i.e. bladder, bowel, womb, etc., it will expel the object causing the swelling, and thus become reduced to its normal size.

The moral content of hexagrams 23 and 15 is, of course, that pride comes before a fall, and that humility leads to being exalted. The pre-heaven hexagram of 15 is 42, Increase, the link between the two being evident.

Metal State of Change

Hexagram 43, Breakthrough (Resoluteness)

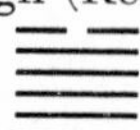

This is the calendar hexagram for the month of April, depicting the time of year in the north when after long struggle, the germinating plants begin to break through the hitherto hampering earth's surface. It refers to life-situations caused by accumulated tension, such as political upheavals; or to a child upon the threshold of youth who is about to break away from the bonds of the nursery and enter the world. In other words, this hexagram depicts a state of change from a sheltered or hidden life which may have become somewhat frustrating or hampering, but which has suddenly been outgrown, or where a breaking-point has been reached. The *I Ching* counsels that arms (which are of metal) should not be resorted to on any account, but that caution and readiness to act at the right time should nevertheless be practised. Metal is the symbol of cutting, and in this sense the hexagram refers to cutting one's way out of a condition, though without the use of violence. In Shao Yung's sequence this hexagram is situated in the south next to hexagram 1, the Creative, that is, it is at the point just before the creative force or forces of light are manifest; or when plant life reaches the earth's surface and sunlight. Its pre-heaven hexagram is 39, Obstruction, which depicts the idea of overcoming barriers and whose connection with the above hexagram is obvious. In this situation, a man is cautioned to withdraw with his weapons in order to study the problem objectively and at a safe distance, so that he may find a road to success and a wise leader to follow.

The other Metal State of Change hexagram is 10, Treading (Conduct), which occupies the position in Shao Yung's sequence directly opposite to hexagram 15, Modesty, of the Earth State of Change, because it has the complementary pattern, thus:

䷉	䷎
hexagram 10	hexagram 15

This hexagram refers to stepping out bravely into life, which it likens to a tiger's tail upon which you may tread if you wish, but that the greatest caution should be exercised in order to prevent yourself from being harmed. It is the natural follow-on after the previous hexagram 43, where you were advised to retire and review the situation carefully before making a breakthrough. Now, hexagram 10 tells you to go forward with courage but at the same time still to avoid rashness.

The pre-heaven hexagram is 4, Youthful Folly, indicating inexperience and the exuberance of youth and picturing the young person or plant hardly ready to deal with the vicissitudes of life, yet wishing to rush headlong into it.

Wood State of Change

Hexagram 42, Increase

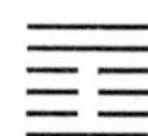

This indicates that the time has come to grow larger and stronger, but that in order that this state may endure it must be accompanied by sharing and sacrifice. A tree puts out branches as it develops, which in turn afford shade for smaller plants. In the human field, the man who establishes himself in a good position in life should share this with others, for example, a wife and family. As a business enterprise expands and flourishes, so more people should be employed and more goods produced to be shared out. The expansion comes about by the reduction of unwanted things, or the sacrifice of Self, which is bound to lead to gain. This is a natural law. As the blossoms at the base of a plant die, so those at the top open.

Wood is the State of Change concerning growth, development and expansion, the pre-heaven hexagram of 42 is 49, Revolution (Moulting), indicating a time of change and of shedding, when the repressions of the past have to be overthrown; a time of metamorphosis in nature, and of revolution in human affairs when the outworn and unwanted are removed.

The second hexagram concerned with the Wood State of Change is 32, Duration

䷟

The meaning of this hexagram has already been dealt with as it is the pre-heaven hexagram of hexagram 23, Splitting Apart. It depicts union as an enduring condition, explaining the need to seek a mate, for pollination, for knowledge to be handed on, in order that life may continue on earth; each producing its own kind either spiritually, mentally or physically, so that there may be continual evolution. However, this can only take place within certain limits, change only manifesting within a state of non-change, perhaps best explained by the planets which move around the sun, yet are held within fixed orbits.

The pre-heaven hexagram of 32 is 38, Opposition, which indicates a condition in which opposites (such as man and woman) are reconciled; in which diverging points of view may be brought together in agreement. This hexagram has to do with the creation and reproduction of life and is the natural precursor to hexagram 32.

Thus we come to the end of the hexagrams which can be formed out of the trigrams composing the Outer States of Change of Earth, Metal and Wood which illustrate the laws of life controlling the time and circumstances when changes can be wrought, either by heaven, earth, conditions, other people, ourselves and so on, whether intentionally or not.

As and when each of these conditions present themselves, or should you wish to create them for a purpose, it would be wise to study the guidance offered by the *I Ching* for behaviour at such times, and as to how such situations can be obtained.

The following is a summary of the foregoing, showing the creation and development of life:

Earth The physical body and the earth-plane.

Hexagram 23. Breaking up of associations, i.e. leaving the

home, nest, etc. to seek a mate. Sex, fertilization and reproduction.

Hexagram 15. Expulsion of fruit, child, etc. Equalization.

Metal Desire to enter into life and the need to think and/or use caution before doing so.

Hexagram 43. Actually breaking out, i.e. a plant reaching the earth's surface; raising things to a climax, causing them to burst; or the avoidance of this.

Hexagram 10. Using courage, but avoiding foolhardiness.

Wood Time of growth and expansion.

Hexagram 42. Sacrificing and spreading the increase.

Hexagram 32. Seeking a mate of one's own kind to ensure continuity of life.

In Shao Yung's sequence the two hexagrams of Earth State of Change are opposite those of the Metal State of Change, whilst those of Wood are opposite to one another, thus:

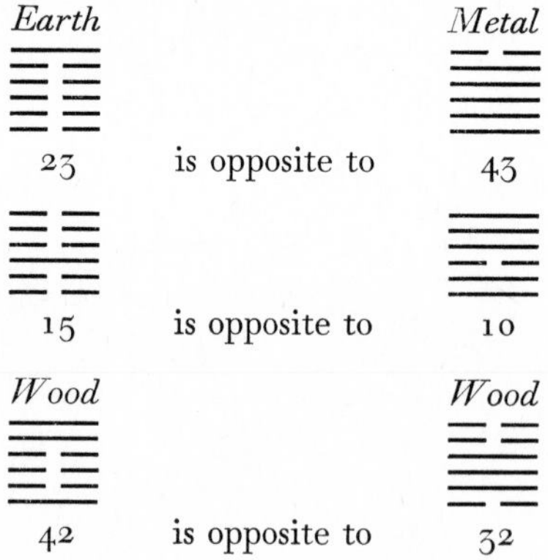

Earth — *Metal*

23 is opposite to 43

15 is opposite to 10

Wood — *Wood*

42 is opposite to 32

(based on Shao Yung's sequence where yang lines are opposite to yin and vice versa).

8 | The magnetic law of the attraction and repulsion of opposite poles, and an explanation of the six spheres of Shao Yung's circular sequence

The geometric progression referred to earlier can perhaps be better understood by studying diagrams 16 and 17 where the hexagrams in Shao Yung's sequence are shown as white and black sections, the six circles representing the six lines of the hexagrams. In the central core of these diagrams T'ai Chi is to be found dwelling in motionless serenity in the same place where, paradoxically, movement commences.

The central portions of these diagrams are half white (left, yang) and half black (right, yin), as are the bottom lines of pre-heaven upon which the diagrams are based. The black half contains a central white streak which indicates the presence of light even where there is the greatest darkness, yang being creative, and yin having no visible life of its own. Progressing outwards into the second circle or the second line of the hexagrams, the division of south/north in the innermost sphere now splits across into a second division running east/west as well. As one moves up through the lines of the hexagrams, the white or black portions increase in number as they begin to split up more and more frequently, until on the perimeter they are alternately white and black. In the outer three circles, which represent the top trigrams of the hexagrams, the white blocks are divided by small black lines, which is not the case with the lower or inner trigrams, indicating that division comes as the result of moving away from the uniting influence of T'ai Chi.

In the exact south on the outermost sphere of diagram 16 there are two white squares next to one another, and in the north two black ones, which illustrates the law of like calling to like or the repulsion of opposites. As soon as this position is arrived at, that is, where there is total light in the south and total darkness in the north, a state of imbalance has been built up to such an extent that by the laws of nature the whole structure must automatically switch into its own opposite (enantiodromia). This is shown in diagram 17 where the hexagrams on the right have become reversed from their previous position in diagram 16, that is, this half of Shao Yung's sequence has become inverted. In other words, a black square has now appeared instead of a white one next to the white in the south and a white next to the black in the north, the two diagrams illustrating the switching of the cosmic forces. It will be observed that it is the right half which changes, that is, the yin, showing the instability of yin and the stability of yang. On the very outside of the circle the white and black squares, which not only alternate but also continually change their nature from positive to negative, and from negative to positive, indicate the disturbing pull, now this way, now that, of the pairs of opposites of physical existence.

In Shao Yung's circular sequence (diagram 11) the lower, inner trigrams are in blocks of eight, whereas the upper outer are set out singly (see *The I Ching and You*, p. 47).

Diagram 18 shows Shao Yung's square sequence, where the hexagrams are still in the same order, the lower or fundamental trigrams being in blocks of eight (as in Shao Yung's circular sequence) when read horizontally, and in singles when read vertically. It is the same case with the upper derived trigrams, which when read horizontally are in single units (as in Shao Yung's circular sequence) and when read vertically are in blocks of eight. This illustrates the criss-cross pattern of life.

Diagrams 19 and 20 will perhaps explain this more clearly. In diagram 19 the lowest (inner) line of pre-heaven is yang on the left and yin on the right, which can be compared with the white or black centres of the circles in diagram 20, where each of the eight figures represents one of the doubled trigram hexagrams. The square blocks beneath each of the circles form the identical pattern in lines instead of curves.

If the reader will go back to diagrams 16 and 17 and concentrate for a few moments on them, he will notice the presence of two interlaced triangles within the pattern, with their apexes south and north. These are, of course, the two triangles of the Chinese cosmos referred to earlier and illustrated in diagram 8.

It was explained in *The I Ching and You* how the lowest line of a hexagram depicts a situation which is only just beginning to form, or into which one has hardly yet entered. This condition then gradually develops through the various lines of the hexagram until the topmost line is reached, indicating the climax or that one is moving out of the situation. There is, therefore, movement from the central point of the circle outwards, during which there is a constant interplay of yang and yin. Having reached the outermost line, the movement can then reverse, that is, the hexagrams can become reversed (which was explained earlier as the reflecting triangles of the Kabbalah), the lowest line becoming the nearest to T'ai Chi.

Occultists declare that the positive and negative forces reverse in the different planes of existence; thus a man is positive and a woman negative on the material plane, whilst on the astral (emotional) plane, the woman becomes positive and the man negative, reversing back again in the lower mental plane and so on, upward.

The functions of the six spheres of Shao Yung's sequence,* read from the outside inwards, which can be taken to represent the six planes of existence, alternating yang and yin, are as follows:

* Suggested by I. and L. E. Mears, *Creative Energy*; see pp. 83–5.

The three spheres denoted by the outer trigram (the Inferior Man)

sphere 1 (sixth or top line of the hexagram): This is the outer circle where yang and yin alternate, where Man is tossed to and fro by opposing forces. It is the place of everyday living; the physical world.
sphere 2 (fifth line of the hexagram): The sphere of feeling or emotion, where Man is beginning to rise above the mundane things of life.
sphere 3 (fourth line of the hexagram): The realm of the intellect which concentrates and is far more serene than the first two, there being less movement between yang and yin.

The three spheres denoted by the inner trigram (the Superior Man)

sphere 4 (third line of the hexagram): The awakening to spiritual consciousness while yet being attracted to the things of earth. The third line of a hexagram is very unstable, being neither spiritual nor material and, as such, usually indicates the weakness in a situation or person depicted by the particular hexagram.
sphere 5 (second line of the hexagram): Rising upward from earthly to higher consciousness.
sphere 6 (first or bottom line of the hexagram): The realization of the one-ness of life. Having attained the innermost sphere, the one nearest to T'ai Chi, it is then necessary for Man to give forth this knowledge to the world by shining down upon it, or descending into it once more; in the same way in which T'ai Chi appears to descend into matter. Man then gradually rises through instinctive action to conscious effort, returning thereby to T'ai Chi, as illustrated by hexagrams 63, 64 and 1, and also by the continual reversing of the hexagrams as shown in King Wên's numerical pairs. The pairs of the

fundamental laws of the universe mentioned earlier (p. 6) tell Man that the strong should support the weak, thus: ⚎; but on the other hand, the weak should follow the strong, thus: ⚍. It is the law of the jungle for the strong to prey upon and destroy the weak, conversely it is natural for a woman to care for her child.

Heaven supports the earth. On the other hand, the earth (female) should follow heaven (male), which could, in a physical sense, be taken to mean the sun. The earth must not reject heaven, but it is the way of yin to reject. The human body (yin) rejects, as today's surgeons performing transplants are too well aware! People who are only interested in physical existence and desire will reject the spiritual; that is why the saints and prophets, not least amongst them Jesus of Nazareth, were, and still are today, rejected by the earth. How many great artists and musicians lived in a garret and were buried in a pauper's grave?

'The devil looks after his own' and 'the good die young' are well-known phrases! Despite their somewhat sarcastic ring, these sayings are true because if a person is of the earth, the earth will support him, but if he be of heaven, he has no real place here. However, the earthly Man must aspire upwards for only then can heaven pour forth its bounty upon him. He must first open the door of his heart before goodness can enter. Heaven will never force itself upon the earth, will never rape, it is therefore for the earth to make the first move. In this chapter I have endeavoured to give a sketch of the general idea behind the complex movement of the hexagrams of the *I Ching*, which work from inside outwards and vice versa; from top to bottom, and bottom to top; turning first this way then that. It is a difficult concept to grasp, inscrutable and full of paradox, but that this is the general pattern of the constantly changing and developing universe, there can be little doubt.

Man must learn to remain very calm amidst all the outer quick-changing yang/yin turmoil surrounding him, withdrawing into the innermost centre of his being (the peaceful yang/yin centre of the circle), there to contact his Maker where all life is one and perfectly still.

Through every vicissitude of life he should avoid action wherever possible, or whenever he is perplexed; but when action is required or deemed necessary for the common good, it must stem from the centre of his being, his higher Self, which rests within T'ai Chi; and not from the lower Self, which is being tossed hither and thither by the outer constantly changing pairs of opposites. He must learn to balance these, taking the golden middle road, avoiding extremes. Such is the philosophy of the *I Ching* and the path of the Superior Man, surely a salient message for the many dissatisfied and lost people of today's restless, violent way of life.

9 | *Mutating hexagrams and the houses of the* I Ching

I recently came across a table of the sixty-four hexagrams from which one is supposed to be able to work out a method of changing one's circumstances. I feel it tends rather to confuse than generally clarify the issue, but that is only my own personal view. Some readers may very well find it of assistance for the purposes of divination or guidance. In any case I feel it would be a pity not to include this because it does undoubtedly make interesting study. Furthermore it was this diagram which gave me the clue to the beginning of an understanding of the eight houses of the *I Ching* about which I had hitherto comprehended nothing. This link-up is explained as the chapter progresses.

Diagram 21* contains thirteen vertical columns in which the hexagrams in the first and last columns are identical in each row, whilst those in the central column (i.e. the seventh) are the exact opposite of these in yang/yin pattern. In other words, after six mutations each hexagram has moved into its own opposite, and then after a further six, making twelve mutations in all, it has returned to its original form; these changes being caused by single lines altering in a rising pattern from the lowest to the topmost. All the hexagrams are contained in this diagram, and appear in the first (and last) column when read vertically. They are in King Wên's numerical sequence which can be taken either in pairs of

* Taken from W. A. Sherrill's *Heritage of Change*; see pp. 81–91.

hexagrams, or in pairs of pairs according to their pattern, as will be explained later. Reading horizontally across the page, it will be noticed that the first two rows (i.e. those commencing with hexagram 1 or hexagram 2) each contain all the calendar hexagrams and therefore are linked to the individual months of the year (see diagram 15). The remaining sixty-two rows of mutations may also have similar links. The twelve columns could very probably have some association with the divisions of the Zodiac. The six mutations could well illustrate the week of six working days, the seventh being omitted because, as a day of rest, all activity (i.e. change) ceases upon it.

Because the sixth mutation contains the exact yang/yin opposite pattern of each hexagram in the first column, this indicates changes wrought by the passage of time (as already illustrated by pre-heaven, Shao Yung's sequence and the calendar hexagrams). In other words, by being read horizontally across the page, the hexagrams indicate time; whereas when read vertically they indicate space, because each column is set out in King Wên's later-heaven sequence. Each row represents a particular cycle so that, when read horizontally from left to right, it reveals how a situation is likely to develop within that cycle. Conversely, when read from right to left, it indicates the seed which caused the present circumstances to have arisen.*

The mutations of these cyclic hexagrams, as with any other hexagrams, can be adjusted or disrupted by Fate, and also to a limited degree by Man himself. Therefore, if you wish to make a change in your circumstances (see p. 73), within a particular cycle, this chart will give general guidance on how this may be attained. For, by selecting the hexagram which most nearly corresponds to your present circumstances, and then finding the one which relates to that state which you wish to achieve, you can work out the necessary mutations which have to be made, and then read the line text of the *I Ching* for the directive to be followed.

* See W. A. Sherrill, *Heritage of Change*, p. 92.

The same, of course, could apply to a change you might wish to make outside a particular cycle, but this would present an enormous and complicated task for you would have to move from one row to another, note the line position where change is or is not to be made, and at the same time ascertain whether this refers to a person, to a situation or other relative factors. Remember that the entire hexagram must be taken into account to calculate the correctness of place and the separate lines to indicate time (see p. 89). It is easy enough to see the pattern the hexagrams have woven *after* the event has taken place because you can then look back and trace all the mutations; but on the other hand it is easier *before* the event to contact the unconscious by means of divination, selecting the correct hexagrams and moving lines, thus guiding yourself in the wisest direction.

Underneath diagram 13 is a table of non-reversible hexagrams which are 1, 2, 27, 28, 29, 30, 61 and 62 which in diagram 21 are above one another in numerical pairs in the first column, i.e. 1 is above 2; 27 above 28; 29 above 30; 61 above 62. They become inverted in the sixth mutation because they are yang/yin opposites line by line (which is seldom the case with King Wên's pairs), for example:

1st column	*7th column (sixth mutation)*
1 } 2	2 } 1
27 } 28	28 } 27
29 } 30	30 } 29

This applies to the following hexagrams (linked together in pairs numerically) as well, which, though not reversible like the above eight, also have opposite yang/yin patterns as follows:

1st column	*7th column (sixth mutation)*
11 } 12	12 } 11
17 } 18	18 } 17
53 } 54	54 } 53
63 } 64	64 } 63

Included in the above-mentioned hexagrams are the doubled-trigram hexagrams of 1, 2, 29 and 30 which concern the forces of yang and yin and the Inner States of Change respectively. However, the remaining doubled-trigram hexagrams, 51, 52, 57 and 58 which contain the Outer States of Change trigrams, mutate in a different fashion, because their yang/yin pattern changes when reversed, thus:

1st column	*7th column (sixth mutation)*
51 } 57	57 } 51
52 } 58	58 } 52

These form blocks of four opposites, that is, a pair of pairs instead of just one pair. In fact all the remaining hexagrams in diagram 16 also mutate in these sets of four, for example:

↑ King Wên (later-heaven) ↓	hexagram 3 } 4	mutates into hexagram 50 } 49;	and 50 } 49	into 3 } 4
	5 } 6	35 } 36;	35 } 36	5 } 6

← Shao Yung (pre-heaven) →

The above mutation of 3 into 50 or 50 into 3, 4 into 49 or 49 into 4, reading across the diagram is concerned with pre-heaven and, therefore, time. On the other hand, the mutation of 3 into 4 or 4 into 3, 50 into 49 or 49 into 50 reading downwards is the concern of later-heaven or place.

Up to the time of studying diagram 21, I had been extremely puzzled by the allocation of the hexagrams into 'houses', as mentioned at the end of the Wilhelm/Baynes translation of the *I Ching*. However, after studying the twelve-stage mutation, I wondered whether there was perhaps an eight-stage mutation which might correspond to the eight houses.

I accordingly set out the hexagrams in columns beginning with the doubled-trigram hexagrams (giving the house name) at the top and placing the other hexagrams in their correct houses in the order given in the *I Ching* (see diagram 22).

A certain pattern of mutation emerged. Reading down the columns it will be found that the hexagrams mutate into one another in much the same fashion as those shown in diagram 21, except that in that case the mutation from one hexagram into another was horizontal, whereas here it is vertical, so that, reading downwards, the second hexagram in each column is formed by the yang/yin change of the bottom line of the first hexagram. Similarly the next hexagram is formed by change in the second line of the previous one. This mutation is continued as far as line five, but does not go further into line six because such a move would change the hexagram into its opposite doubled-trigram pattern and this would switch it into a different house. For example, in the Creative house (row six) hexagram 23 ☶☷ would become hexagram 2 ☷☷ were the top line to change, but hexagram 2 belongs to the Receptive house, and this does not therefore occur.

In the seventh row the mutation reverts back from line five to line four. Why this is so I am at present at a loss to understand. Maybe it has been explained in some as yet untranslated or unavailable Chinese book. Nor do I know why this repeated movement in line four, which is the lowest line of the top trigram, should cause the entire bottom trigram to change into its complete opposite in row eight; a fifth line change in row eight bringing the hexagram back to its doubled-trigram house pattern in row one. It will be noted that the Creative and Receptive houses contain all the positive and negative calendar hexagrams respectively, that is six in each column; and, due to the repeated fourth and fifth line changes, the later-heaven counterparts of the Creative and Receptive trigrams, that is Fire and Water, are introduced as top trigrams.

In relation to cosmic unfolding, the meaning of each of the houses is given by the *I Ching*, as follows:

house 1, *the Creative*

God battles and struggles in the Creative.

house 2, *the Abysmal*

God toils in the Abysmal.

house 3, *the Keeping Still*

God completes the work of the year and brings all living things to perfection in the Keeping Still.

house 4, *the Arousing*

God comes forth to his producing work in the Arousing, and reveals himself in Thunder.

house 5, *the Gentle*

God brings his processes into full and equal action and completes them in the Gentle.

house 6, *the Clinging*

God's processes are manifested to one another in the Clinging, which causes creatures to perceive each other.

house 7, *the Receptive*

God causes things to serve one another in the Receptive which is where the greatest service is done for God.

house 8, *the Joyous*

God rejoices in the Joyous.

10 | The lines of a hexagram

In *The I Ching and You* it was pointed out in relation to divining that every line of a hexagram cast in answer to a question has a bearing upon it, but that the moving lines are of the greatest importance for they contain the directive to be followed. Formed out of the first hexagram, because usually there are moving lines, is a second hexagram, all the lines of which are of consequence. Those occupying analogous positions with the moving lines of the first hexagram are again the most important. So it is that every line of both the hexagrams, whether moving or static, has a direct reference to the situation in question.

Every hexagram can be read either way up (see p. 62), because each hexagram contains within itself both yang and yin lines (with the exception of hexagrams 1 and 2 which individually represent the mighty force of yang or yin alone and in their purest form, yet even these contain the seeds of the opposite influence). It is necessary intuitively to pick up the yang or yin, to feel with regard to it a 'pull' in either direction affecting the entire answer. This is the reason why it is difficult for the *I Ching* to be used by a diviner who is subjectively involved in the case, it being almost impossible under such circumstances to subdue the desires of the lower mind.

In the *I Ching* the meeting of yang and yin is associated with falling rain which is the very lifeblood of this planet, and therefore is, as water is, the first State of Change. An example will be found in hexagram 43 where lines 3 and 6 are proper correlates.*

There is a mutual communication between pairs of opposites as follows:

yin yang	of heaven
malevolence benevolence	of Man
soft hard	of earth

It is important to realize that in addition to standing for heaven, pre-heaven and unseen thought, yang also denotes *time*. In the same way yin, besides meaning earth, later-heaven and tangible things, is also the symbol for *space*. The *I Ching*† explains this by saying that because of the unity of the hexagram of the Creative, the individual lines stand in a continuous relationship that, as it progresses, clarifies the idea of the whole still further. In this respect the Creative forms a contrast to the Receptive, in which the single lines stand side by side without inner relationship. This inheres in the *temporal* character of the Creative as contrasted with the *spatial* character of the Receptive.

Thus the *separate lines* of a hexagram indicate *time*; *pre-heaven* also indicates *time*. This is why the pre-heaven arrangement of the trigrams forms the basis of Shao Yung's circular sequence which is concerned with the calendar hexagrams, the months and the seasons (see chapter 7).

Because, as just explained, the individual lines of yin stand side by side without inner relationship, the hexagram *taken as a whole* indicates *space* (as against *the individual lines* representing *time*). Therefore the hexagrams of King Wên (based

* See James Legge's translation of the *I Ching*, notes under hexagram 43, p. 154.

† See the Wilhelm/Baynes translation of the *I Ching*, Book 3, The Commentaries (d)5, p. 378.

on his later-heaven trigram arrangement) in the numerical order of the text of *I Ching*, *when taken in their entirety*, refer to *space* or *place*. The following table will clarify:

Time	*Space and place*
yang, heaven, thought	yin, earth, matter
unseen things	manifested life
individual lines of hexagram	hexagram in its entirety
pre-heaven trigrams	later-heaven trigrams
Shao Yung's sequence (which shows the cause of seasonal change)	Numerical sequence of hexagrams in text of *I Ching* (denotes actual physical phenomena)

Yang is movement and unites with ease what is divided. It is effortless because it guides positively, particularly when things are smallest; this is why the *I Ching* stresses the importance of recognizing evil and stamping it out at the very beginning before it has had time to grow into something too big to direct into positive channels. The direction of yang determines in the germinal stage of doing, causing everything to develop quite effortlessly of itself according to its own nature. Therefore the inner movement must be in harmony with the environment and the cosmic laws. Yin is reposed and simple, and this simplicity which arises out of pure receptivity becomes the germ of existence. It is only through receptivity of the earth that a seed can germinate; it is only through the receptivity of a woman that a child can be conceived; and through the mind that inspiration may be absorbed.

The corresponding lines of the upper and lower trigrams do not stand in the relationship of correspondence* in any hexagram formed out of the doubling of a trigram, namely ䷳ or ䷝, etc. because they are always either both yang

* Lines 1 and 4; 2 and 5; 3 and 6 correspond. One should be yang and the other yin. See *The I Ching and You*, p. 62.

or both yin.* When misfortune is said to 'come from without' it means it has happened as the result of heaven's will; 'misfortune from within' being the outcome of our own specific fault. Sometimes this is shown as the outer (upper) and inner (lower) trigrams respectively, a clear example being in the text of hexagram 5, where the trigram for danger ☵ is outside (upper trigram):

☵ outside (upper)
☰ inside (lower)

showing in this particular case that the danger or misfortune is from without, that is, brought about by the action of Fate.

There are said to be about 500 ways to obtain an oracle, but all can be classified into ten categories (the number of the earth and of completion). The coin or stalk method is sufficient for most people.

There is the *I Ching* of Buddhism and the *I Ching* of Taoism, and it is difficult not to become confused as one studies various different approaches to this vast subject.

There are three types of change in the *I Ching*: 1. non-change; 2. cyclic change; 3. sequent change, which are explained as follows:

1. This is the fixed point to which change can be referred. It is the *decision* and refers to pre-heaven, in which mankind is already enclosed. A point of reference must be chosen to coincide with the cosmic forces, otherwise everything in life will become ruined, broken up and chaotic. This is an explanation of the use of the word *decision*.

2. This is organic physical life and material things which, having a life cycle, are born, mature and die. It refers to later-heaven.

3. This is the onward-moving process which never returns to the starting-point, i.e. the succession of the generations.

Change can, of course, be disrupted by Fate in order to make corrections.

* See the *I Ching* (Wilhelm/Baynes translation), p. 654; commentary on the Image of hexagram 52.

An ancient and as yet untranslated Chinese book gives a slightly different method from usual of interpreting the moving lines, which may be of assistance to some readers but not to all. By all means adopt it if you find it helpful, otherwise carry on with the method outlined in *The I Ching and You* or with any other method you may have employed up to this time, bearing in mind that you make your own arrangement with the unconscious (see *The I Ching and You*, p. 30), it being essential not to confuse the communication already established by making too many alterations to it.

One of the main arguments I have against this particular method is that, as shown below, in the case where all six lines move and the text of the second hexagram only is to be taken, the position would appear to be similar to, if not actually identical with, that of a locked hexagram, so I do not quite see the point of the unconscious having directed the throwing of the first hexagram which, if it is to be ignored, is surely superfluous. Unless possibly the first hexagram is to be used to point out something significant which has led up to the present circumstances.

The interpretation is as follows:

one moving line take the meaning of this line.

two moving lines when there is a nine and a six take the six to explain.

Where both are nines or sixes, take the upper moving line.

three moving lines explain by the text of the middle moving line.

four moving lines explain by the text of the upper static line, namely:

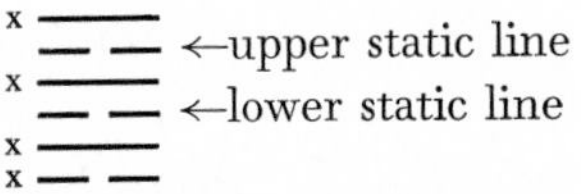

```
x ———
  — —  ←upper static line
x ———
  — —  ←lower static line
x ———
x — —
```

(x expresses the moving lines)

five moving lines explain by the text of the static line (there is only one).

six moving lines in hexagram 1 use the text of 'nine for all six places'. In hexagram 2 use the text of 'six for all six places'. For all the other hexagrams, judge by the text and commentaries of the second hexagram.

no moving lines explain by the text and commentary of that hexagram.

Each line of a hexagram can be taken to represent a period of two months, the entire hexagram therefore representing one year, but this is by no means a hard and fast rule. A table showing the specific years to which each hexagram belongs is given in *The I Ching and You* (p. 85).

I have found from personal experience that asking several questions on the same subject, but phrased in different ways, can often be of the greatest value in clarifying the position. For example, you might enquire: 'Should I change my job?' If the answer is not quite clear, you could then ask two questions: 'Please give the general picture of what the position will be if I do change my job', and '. . . if I do *not* change my job.' Compare the last two answers with one another, and then with the first one.

Remember that the *I Ching* must only be used for guidance and not for fortune-telling.

The formation of the wording of the question is important. For example, when seeking guidance over a career, you could ask, '*Should* I take up art?' The *I Ching* might say, 'Yes', knowing full well that it might be excellent for you to make an effort and to overcome many difficulties in order to do so, but nevertheless the road might be very thorny in the process. Of course all this will be revealed in the hexagram if it is properly analysed. If, however, the question is rephrased as, '*Could* I take up art?', the *I Ching* will indicate whether or not you have the ability to do so, but it might not necessarily be the best thing for you to do.

When interpreting a hexagram it is, therefore, important to bear in mind the actual phrasing used in the question, otherwise the answers can become twisted and muddled. If the answers to the above questions are either affirmative or negative you will have an even clearer answer and general picture of the position than if only one had been asked. One question is very rarely sufficient, unless the matter is very straightforward and simple.

The identical question must, of course, never be asked more than once as this implies a lack of faith on the part of the diviner which will consequently block the working of the unconscious. It is also important not to go on continually asking about a problem until the *I Ching* appears to give an answer which coincides with personal desires.

Remember also, when interpreting a hexagram, to analyse the line position (see *The I Ching and You*, p. 61), and take into account the nuclear trigrams and hexagrams involved (ibid., p. 75). Sometimes a good deal of light can be shed upon a problem by asking the *I Ching* about any possible Karmic links which may be pertinent. These will be revealed immediately, and particularly by the hexagram's pre-heaven counterpart, for the balancing condition of these trigrams (where yang is opposite to yin, and yin to yang) illustrates the very nature of Karma which, by its reciprocal action, heaps upon the head of the wrongdoer or the saint, the evil or blessing which he has given forth to another, whether by thought, or its outcome, deed.

11 | *Astrology*

Diagram 23 shows the signs of the Zodiac in the order normal to astrologers, together with the trigrams of the *I Ching* concerning each of them. Diagram 24 shows the hexagrams in Shao Yung's sequence with their Zodiac counterparts. You may refer to whichever diagram you prefer depending upon whether you are an astrologer or a person more acquainted with the *I Ching*.

Those readers who have a thorough understanding of the characteristics of the trigrams of the *I Ching* and the signs of the Zodiac may be puzzled by the apparently strange relationship in meaning between many of the pairs; the most startling perhaps being the dynamic Aries and the gentle, submissive Wind, Aries being anything but submissive! I shall endeavour to explain the reason for the apparent discrepancies as this chapter unfolds.

In order to understand the general tie-up which exists between these two great branches of occultism it should be realized that whilst the signs of the Zodiac are linked with the four elements, the *I Ching* trigrams are not so much elements as states of change of which there are five instead of four. These depict the four seasons (spring, summer, autumn and winter) and the earth, as follows:

summer
spring earth autumn
winter

(cf. later-heaven diagram in *The I Ching and You*).

The Zodiac also proceeds from one sign (i.e. one month) to

the next, season by season, merging from one element into another, and it is through the changes which take place when this happens that the link between astrology and the *I Ching* occurs. Therefore, if the reader can move away from the concept of astrological signs indicating personal characteristics or specific happenings, and delve deeper into this great science which deals just as much with the balancing of the pairs of opposites as does the *I Ching*, he will be able to find the link-up between the two.

For example, returning once more to Aries and the Wind, Aries is the starter of things, and as such is the first sign of the Zodiac series. The trigram of the Wind represents the number five (change) which dwells in the centre of the tortoise and moves to the south-west position in pre-heaven. It is the first trigram after the great yang/yin switch of cosmic energy, and as a pioneering force, therefore, its action can be as dynamic and originating as Aries.

I Ching State of Change	*trigram*	*half Zodiac sign*	*element*	*full Zodiac sign*	*element*
Metal	☱	Leo (fixed)	fire	Virgo (mutable)	earth
	☰	Scorpio (fixed)	water	Libra (cardinal)	air
Wood	☴	Taurus (fixed)	earth	Aries (cardinal)	fire
	☳	Aquarius (fixed)	air	Pisces (mutable)	water
Earth	☶	Aquarius (fixed)	air	Capricorn (cardinal)	earth
	☷	Leo (fixed)	fire	Cancer (cardinal)	water
Fire	☲	Taurus (fixed)	earth	Gemini (mutable)	air
Water	☵	Scorpio (fixed)	water	Sagittarius (mutable)	fire

The reason why certain signs have been allocated to particular trigrams is best explained by placing the *I Ching* States of Change with them as shown on p. 95.

From this table it will be seen that:

1. All the fixed signs are divided into two as the result of *I Ching* change, that is, at the moment of greatest inertia movement (change) takes place (see diagrams 23 and 24).

2. Each *I Ching* State of Change contains Zodiac elements of earth, air, fire and water (two half signs and two complete signs).

3. Besides the fixed signs mentioned in 1 above, the top two States of Change, namely Metal and Wood, contain both

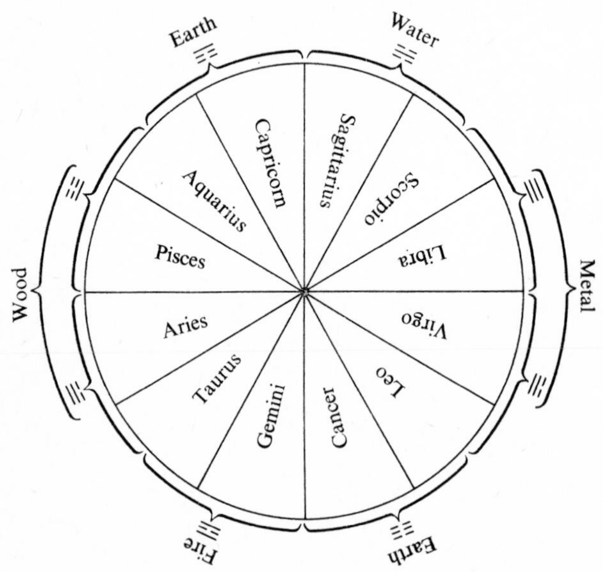

mutable and cardinal signs, whereas the Earth State of Change, which can be split into two halves, contains in each half one cardinal sign only; whilst Fire and Water, which are separate States of Change, contain only one mutable sign each.

By placing the States of Change around the Zodiac circle, it can be seen in the figure on p. 96 how the *I Ching* is based upon the Zodiac, the trigram of Water being opposite Fire, next to the divided Earth, with Wood in the east and Metal in the west.

Diagram 25 shows the trigrams arranged in later-heaven. If the signs of the Zodiac and the States of Change related to each, as shown in the previous figure, are placed in this order, they will be seen to coincide with the Yellow River States of Change (diagram 6), which is based upon later-heaven trigrams whose link-up with River Lo, pre-heaven and the tortoise has already been pointed out (see chapter 4).

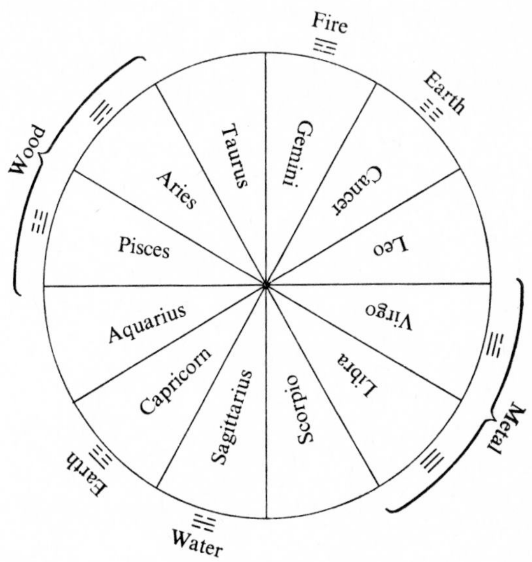

Comparing this figure with the previous one, it will be noticed that Fire is now above Water, that is, hexagram 63 ䷾ has become hexagram 64 ䷿; also Fire and Water have reversed positions with the Earth. In other words the two diagrams have become reflections of one another as far as the Inner States of Change and the Earth are concerned.

The divided fixed signs are equidistant from one another, both in the *I Ching* and the Zodiac circles. In astrology these particular four signs have been called the four pillars of the earth, the *I Ching* explanation of this being that because their positions form an × this is identical with the black dot formation of River Lo. They are therefore yin and of the earth, thus:

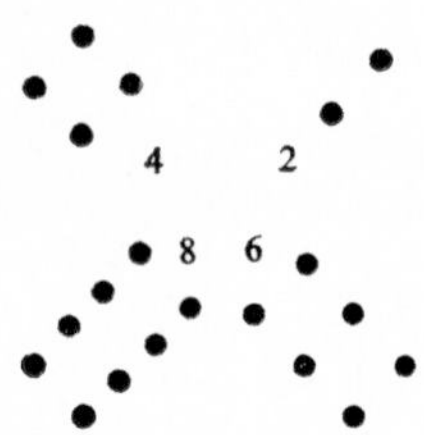

In diagram 24, which deals with pre-heaven, each of these four fixed signs, which are the only ones to be split up and changed, comes under one of the four trigrams principally concerned with change (as well as one of the other four trigrams which need not concern us here), as follows:

sign	*element*	*trigram of change*
Taurus (negative)	earth	the Wind (number 5 at the centre of the tortoise)
Leo (positive)	fire	the Receptive (negative cosmic force)
Scorpio (negative)	water	the Creative (positive cosmic force)
Aquarius (positive)	air	the Arousing (trigram of movement)

The above figure shows the positive and negative of yang and yin influence as follows: Taurus (negative) and Leo (positive);

also Scorpio (negative) and Aquarius (positive) working together in pairs of opposites. Whilst the top two trigrams, Wind (daughter) and the Receptive (mother), are negative, the remaining two, the Creative (father) and the Arousing (son), are positive,* bringing in a criss-cross reciprocal influence. As the previous figure shows, each of these particular signs belongs to one of the four elements.

Each element is associated with three Zodiac signs, each of which is either fixed, cardinal or mutable in nature, thus:

air	*fire*	*water*	*earth*	
Aquarius	Leo	Scorpio	Taurus	*fixed*
Gemini	Sagittarius	Pisces	Virgo	*mutable*
Libra	Aries	Cancer	Capricorn	*cardinal*

(see diagram 26)

The above four fixed signs form cornerstones of support, guarding and conserving what has been started, seeing that things are done, altering their original fixed attitudes of, to Will (Leo), to Dare (Scorpio), to Know (Aquarius) and to Keep Silent (Taurus),† bringing them into manifestation. The actual *fixed* sign itself is resistant to change, signifying fixity of purpose, but which, at this very moment, according to the trigrams of the *I Ching*, becomes the point of movement through the process of enantiodromia.

In diagram 24 (which deals with pre-heaven) or 25 (which deals with later-heaven), the eight trigrams occupy five degrees within each of the Zodiac signs, for example, Thunder is 6°–10° of Pisces, between hexagram 42 (which is 0°–5°) and hexagram 51 (11°–15°). However, the four

* These four trigrams never change their sex, whether in pre-heaven or later-heaven (see p. 39).

† The qualifications necessary for the neophyte on 'the Path' (see J. Krishnamurti, *At the Feet of the Master*).

signs Taurus, Aquarius, Scorpio and Leo, because they are fixed, do not carry any of the trigrams (agents of change) within them. Thus the importance of these four particular signs with regard to change and non-change and their link as such with pre-heaven and later-heaven arrangements of the *I Ching* can be seen.

Biblical symbolism makes an interesting reference to these in a vision seen by the prophet Ezekiel,* which first alludes to 'many wheels', which are most probably the circle of the Zodiac and the several circular arrangements of the *I Ching*;† then the vision continues with a description of four beasts as follows: 'As for the likeness of their faces, they four had the face of a man, and the face of a lion, on the right side: and they four had the face of an ox on the left side; they four also had the face of an eagle.' The 'man' is Aquarius the Water-carrier, whose opposite sign Leo is 'a lion'; whilst 'an ox' is the bull, Taurus. Lastly, mention is made of 'an eagle', which, as astrologers know, is another name for Scorpio, because this is the sign of the sinner or the saint, the one who crawls upon the earth as a scorpion or mounts towards heaven as an eagle.

The symbols of these four Zodiac signs are also contained in the Egyptian sphynx, which has the head of a man, the body of a lion, the wings of an eagle and the tail of an ox.

In his book *Jupiter: The Preserver*, Alan Leo refers (in Lecture 2) to the earth living through seven rounds within which are the seven root races and seven sub-races, a theory well-known to Theosophists.

This number seven is based astrologically on the triplicities, that is, the four elements, earth, air, fire and water, and the quadruplicities, cardinal, mutable and fixed, making seven divisions in all. However, all these divisions need not concern us here; it is only necessary to know that at the present moment humanity is evolving through the fourth round which is engaged in the work of struggle, forming manifold

* See Ezekiel, 1:10.

† Could possibly also refer to the cycles of incarnation.

relations between spirit and matter, symbolized by the Permanent Cosmic *fixed* Cross whose influence remains for many millions of years. The series of the seven crosses which symbolize the whole process of involution and evolution are as follows:

involution

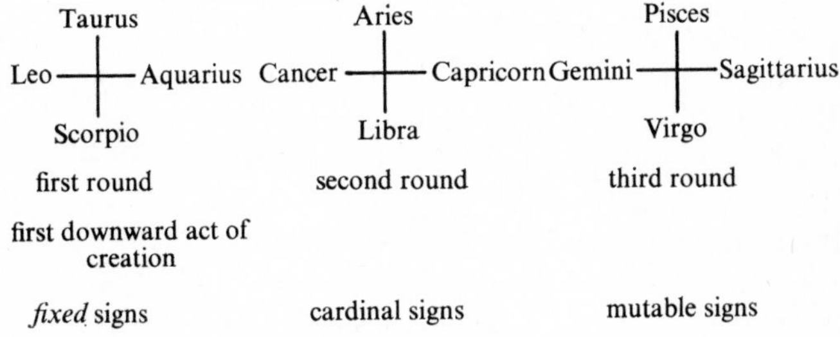

qualities imparted to matter

evolution

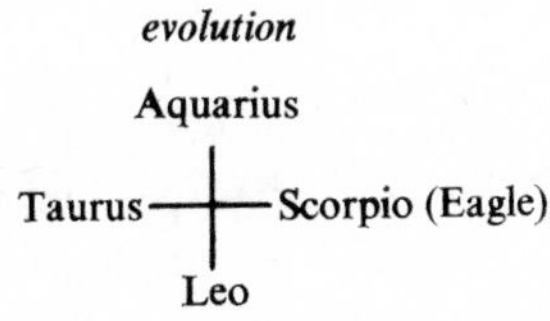

fourth round

struggle between spirit and matter
humanity's present position
fixed signs

(*Note:* This figure is taken from *Jupiter: The Preserver* by Alan Leo.)

The above figures show how, besides the fourth round in which Man exists at present, the first and final acts of creation of our present era are concerned with the fixed signs of the Zodiac. The *I Ching* has obviously, therefore, been given as guidance for this particular period which, as already just mentioned, lasts many millions of years.

Every twelve months the sun moves through all the Zodiac signs, and the world completes one hexagram of the *I Ching* (see *The I Ching and You*, p. 85). It takes 26,000 years for it to move through the entire Zodiac cycle, but only sixty years to complete the *I Ching* hexagram sequence—sixty instead of sixty-four because the hexagrams at the cardinal points, namely 1, 2, 29 and 30, are omitted, as the trigrams of Fire (hexagram 30) and Water (hexagram 29) deal with the Inner States of Change and are not so much concerned with time, being omitted from the calendar hexagrams. Fire and Water refer to Man's evolution within himself of which the Creative (hexagram 1) and the Receptive (hexagram 2) are the pre-heaven counterparts.

At the bottom of diagram 24 there is a small figure which shows that when the hexagrams of the *I Ching* are placed in Shao Yung's sequence (pre-heaven), thus splitting the four fixed Zodiac signs into separate portions, the degrees of the signs no longer read in an orderly sequence, i.e. are no longer 0°–5°, 6°–10° and so on around the circle as they are in diagrams 23 and 25, but instead the sequence order is reversed at the south and north poles, i.e. at yang and yin, and also at the points south-west and north-west, as indicated in the small diagram. These are the exact positions where the Creative and Receptive are formed in King Wên's later-heaven trigram arrangement, and therefore the Zodiac is the bridge between Shao Yung's circular sequence and King Wên's numerical sequence, that is, between pre-heaven and later-heaven.

It is not possible to make any really deep, serious study of the *I Ching* without a certain amount of basic knowledge of astrology, the one being interwoven within the other.

The months of the year as given in the text of the *I Ching*, or by the hexagrams based upon them such as the calendar ones, may be taken to indicate the correct time for the purposes of divination, for they coincide with the Zodiac sign to a certain extent but, as already mentioned, those readers living in the southern hemisphere should remember that the seasons, and not the months, should be reversed, i.e. 'summertime' means 'wintertime'; but 'June' means 'June'. (See *The I Ching and You*, p. 26.) Naturally, you never reverse the wording of the text of the hexagram.

12 | *Healing and health*

According to the *I Ching* the condition of any manifesting phenomenon (later-heaven) is the direct result of thought (pre-heaven). If this is so, then our physical bodies, together with their resistance or otherwise to illness and injury, must also be the outcome of thought. Thought is therefore fundamentally important to health. This is not to say that sickness is all in the mind, but rather that the mind obviously must influence the general pattern of physical well-being. For instance, it is common knowledge that the emotions of fear or excitement have a marked effect upon the mechanics of the body.

As with everything else in the universe, a state of equilibrium has to be achieved between opposing extremes both in, as well as around, the human body. For example, too much heat or cold, under normal conditions, can lead to discomfort or trouble; a chemical and cell imbalance can be dangerous, and so on.

Until Man's archetypal pattern is changed *by him* he will continue to be susceptible to the workings of microbes, bacteria and all other unpleasant manifestations of this type. Until such time, therefore, he will have to fill himself up with pills and spend endless sessions with the doctor. His children and children's children will continue to live in this fashion until the hereditary tendencies of thousands of years of wrong, unbalanced thinking have been completely eradicated, and through harmonious and right thought a new archetype has emerged which will be totally immune to ill-health, no matter to what extent it be surrounded by germs.

Quite often people who appear to be very negative or even perhaps full of evil ways, enjoy abundant good health, whilst those harbouring positive and good thoughts are sick. In the latter case it is because they have inherited a weak or sickly body and their positive thoughts have not yet been able to counteract this defect, but it is certain that future generations are bound to benefit by this harmonious thought. The fact that one does or does not inherit a strong body may be the result of Karma.

Problems relating to health are extremely difficult to solve by means of the *I Ching*. Nevertheless questions can be asked as to what is causing the particular imbalance, and what the cure should be (two separate questions, of course), but the answer will probably be very difficult to interpret. For this reason some western scholars of the *I Ching* suggest that it is easier, and therefore generally more accurate, to use astrology rather than the *I Ching* to diagnose illness, for whilst there are over 10,000 written commentaries on healing by means of the *I Ching*, few if any of these have as yet been translated from the original Chinese. In any case these methods are very difficult to understand, the instruction having to be given by a great master who has profound knowledge and experience.

One of the methods of approach to this is through the art of acupuncture which is based upon the yang/yin principles of the *I Ching*. In his book, *What is Acupuncture?*, Dr E. W. Stiefvater states that the balance of energy in the human body equals how much the activity of the hollow and dense organs (yang and yin) are in harmony with each other; and that each organ has 'intelligence' within itself.

Diagram 27, which is taken from Dr Stiefvater's book, shows the Chinese organ clock of twenty-four hours from which, to use a few examples, the following may be noted:

5–7 a.m. the large intestine acts.

1–3 p.m. after the midday meal a phase of fatigue sets in.

3 a.m. most cases of death occur because of low blood pressure and reduced heart function.

If a person wakes regularly between one and three a.m., it is a pointer to a disturbed function of the liver. Wrong timing of bowel movement indicates trouble in that particular direction. The liver is said to be the seat of the unconscious. Grief, worry, sorrow, anger and anxiety can damage this organ which in turn affects moods, forming a vicious circle.

You have to get to know your own built-in clock and heed its warnings.

Lists of the parts of the body and the trigrams associated with each with regard to health are contained in *The I Ching and You* (see pp. 116 and 117), and also in W. A. Sherrill's book, *Heritage of Change*.

As already mentioned, the left side of the body is yang and the right yin (see p. 55), therefore the left side of a man's body is important, and the right of a woman's, and is the side on which treatment, for example injections, should be given. The following is a table showing the difference between various yang and yin parts of the body which may be helpful for diagnosis:

Yang: hollow organs which are of movement (peristaltic) (see p. 89), active, eliminating (centrifical). Stomach, small intestine, large intestine, gall bladder.

Yin: the dense organs, massive, sluggish, 'dark'. Liver, kidneys, heart, spleen, pancreas, lungs.

(*Note:* the heart and blood-vessels are not regarded as hollow because they are co-ordinated with blood and therefore yin, as is blood itself, because blood is mass and does not move of itself.)

13 | *A comparison between the* I Ching, *the Ten Commandments, numerology and the Tarot greater arcana*

It is necessary to understand the occult meaning of numbers before one can fully appreciate the esoteric application of the tortoise diagram of the *I Ching* (see diagram 3) which concerns the realms of thought or spirit, which is pre-heaven. For this reason this chapter, which relates to various branches of occultism and their similar number symbolisms, is included. This subject was touched upon in chapter 2 which described my visit to an African witchdoctor and pointed out how different nationalities or religious groups are linked together by various philosophies and mysteries, unknowingly, despite vast distances and contrasting cultures.

Whilst it may be intensely interesting to study numerous forms of divining and their related numerical symbolism, it is important not to lose sight of the fact that to employ more than one method at a time will undoubtedly confuse the link with the unconscious and the development of the intuition. Rather, therefore, should you find the particular method which has the strongest appeal for you, and with which you can develop the greatest success, and use this only in order to establish your unconscious to conscious symbolic code, as mentioned in the introduction to this book and also in *The I Ching and You*.

The various occult branches have been grouped under their specific number* and their relative compound numbers, for

* See F. Homer Curtiss, *The Key to the Universe*; A. E. Waite, *The Key to the Tarot* and L. H. Cheiro, *Cheiro's Book of Numbers*.

example: ten, being one and zero, adds up to one, and is therefore classified under the number one. Note that there is a positive and/or negative aspect to each number.

One

I Ching: the Creative ☰, the unbroken line of yang, symbolizing singleness, union, success. As the father aspect of the trinity of the Godhead, it symbolizes power, male, goodness, success and heaven.
Tortoise: the tail which balances the body and, like a rudder, determines the direction, representing the path of life and singleness of purpose.
Kabbalah: Kether, the Crown.
Commandment: 'Thou shalt have no other Gods before me.' This does not necessarily refer only to the making of images, but that Man must not make a god of money, sex, another person or any other thing he desires. The number one represents the omnipotence of God.
Tarot: 'the Magician'. A symbol of power and the will; male.
Numerology: originality, individualization, a person standing on their own.
Glyph: | (one person, alone).

Compound number ten is placed here as an extension of one as it is considered in occultism, as explained above. Ten is the number of completion. There are ten *Chakras* or psychic centres, though only seven concern humanity at the moment. There are suspected to be ten planets, the tenth already having been named Vulcan, though only nine have so far been discovered.
Kabbalah: Malkuth, the kingdom, the reflection of the number one.
Commandment: as ten is the number of completion, the last of the Commandments says: 'Thou shalt not covet . . .'. When

Man reaches completion, everything is his, therefore there is nothing to covet. As long as there is lust after anything, there cannot be completion.
Tarot: 'the Wheel of Fortune'. This is the circle of life which goes first upwards then downwards as it rotates; standing for destiny, the cycle of necessity and the reincarnating ego.
Numerology: completion and perfection.

Glyph: **1** and **0**. As this is a compound number of one, though on a higher cycle, it contains a circle which is a continuous line, ending where it began, symbolizing the finished act; and also the presence of spirit, which is without beginning or end.

Nineteen is a further extension of one and also, therefore, of ten.
Tarot: 'the Sun', the creative power of the solar system.
Numerology: success, honours and happiness.

Glyph: **1** and **9**. The circle has a tail, showing that it has left the previous position and has risen higher.

Further extensions of the number ten are, of course, twenty-eight, thirty-seven and so on. However, as the tortoise diagram refers only to the trump numbers of the greater arcana of the Tarot, and as this is not a book on numerology, the higher numbers do not concern us.

Two

I Ching and Tortoise: the Lake ☱, which is the symbol for the mouth, representing the giving forth of knowledge and the dispersal of intelligence. Its negative side is talkativeness and gossip, or, as the trigram for joy, it can depict lust.

In the tortoise two represents the right paw, the place of the honoured guest, a position of importance. The right hand is normally the strongest.
Kabbalah: Chokmah, wisdom.
Commandment: 'Thou shalt not make unto thee any graven

image of any thing that is in the earth.' As with the first Commandment this does not necessarily refer to idols, but rather that material things must never be allowed to become a substitute for God. This Commandment goes on to say that God is jealous, meaning that nothing must be allowed to stand between Man and the Divine. Man continually seeks for happiness in material possessions or in people around him, but because these are of the earth, they are merely temporary, eventually becoming worn out, lost or dead (referring only to the physical body of a person, of course). In this way, the 'jealous' Divine teaches Man to seek only for the eternal.

Two represents the feminine aspect of the Godhead, the Holy Spirit who endows with wisdom, and, in the form of conscience, is the disperser of spiritual knowledge upon earth.
Tarot: 'the Priestess'. The mother influence and a virgin, for example Mary of the Christians, Kuan Yin of the Chinese or Isis of the Egyptians. This trump stands for a woman, mystery, secrets, wisdom, inspiration and science.
Numerology: association (one and one make two), duality, adaptation, the passive principle of opposition.
Glyph: **2**. Half a circle, therefore only partially complete, but joined to the horizontal one, with which it is associated.

Eleven is the first compound number of two.
Tarot: 'Strength', meaning fortitude. It symbolizes occult power which is more than mere physical strength, representing union with the Divine. It shows a person who has great difficulties to contend with, but who eventually wins esteem. As mentioned above, the number two depicts the right hand of strength.
Numerology: eleven is one of the so-called 'master' numbers, symbolizing occult powers; also idealism of a rather impractical and visionary type.

Twenty is the second compound number of two, and is omitted from the tortoise diagram as there are only two

numbers associated with each section. However, as it is one of the Tarot trumps, it is included here.
Tarot: 'the Last Judgment', representing eternal life and the fulfilment of having listened to the dictates of conscience (number two) and the second Commandment.
Numerology: a call to action to some purpose and the awakening of new ideas.

Three

I Ching and Tortoise: Fire ☲, the Clinging. The combining of yang and yin; the physical enclosed by the spiritual; consciousness. The fire of sacrificial cleansing, of enlightenment and manifested beauty. The intuition.
Kabbalah: Binah, understanding, beauty.
Commandment: 'Thou shalt not take the name of the Lord thy God in vain.' This shows that the power of God on earth must never be invoked for selfish purposes. It is a warning against black magic, the black Mass, prayer for the elevation of self, restriction of other people, and, in fact, any selfish or evil purpose. It represents the father/mother aspect of the Godhead upon earth, that is, God the Son, omnipotent, omnipresent and omniscient love. It is symbolic of the sacrifice of God into the limitation of matter which is the true occult and inner meaning of the Christian Eucharist, the Christ often being referred to as the Light of the World, the sun (trigram of Fire), considered by primitive Man to be the manifestation of God.
Tarot: 'the Empress', which symbolizes fecundity and the gateway of birth and death, hence the great importance attached to the birth and death of Jesus.
Numerology: self-expression, the artist, the joy-giver, the maker of beauty.
Glyph: **3**. Two half-circles one above the other, symbolizing the circle of heaven joined to the lower circle of the earth.

Twelve is the first compound number of three.

Tarot: 'the Hanged Man', which signifies sacrifice, but with deep entrancement, not suffering.
Numerology: sacrifice, the victim, possibly of plots made by other people; worry, also self-sacrifice, which, when linked with God the Son (as mentioned in three, above) explains the Christian Eucharist sacrifice symbolism.

Twenty-one is the second compound number of three which is also not found in the tortoise diagram, but included nevertheless in the Tarot trumps and therefore mentioned here.
Tarot: 'the World' or 'the Crown of the Magi'. It stands for the rapture of the world in God; for a crown of success and honours which are only achieved after a long fight and tests of determination.
Numerology: a fortunate number of promise of success and honours.

Four

I Ching and Tortoise: the Arousing, Thunder ☳, quickening energy, the birth of living things upon earth, the start of a project, etc.
Kabbalah: Chesed or Gedulah, mercy.
Commandment: 'Six days shalt thou work, and rest upon the seventh.' The trinity of the Godhead, seen in the first three numbers, now descends into matter, this number standing for physical plane existence. The Commandment lays down instructions as to when Man should work and for how long he should rest. The recuperative power of the regularly returning sabbath rest refreshes and quickens him ready for the following week's work. The Commandment also refers to rest being taken by: 'sons and daughters', who represent the positive and negative (yang and yin) aspects of thought; 'man and maidservant', referring to the positive and negative aspects of work; 'cattle', depicting the lower animal Self which must also cease its activities, for the 'day must be kept holy'.

Tarot: 'the Emperor', which represents the positive aspect of 'the Empress' (see Tarot number three), with the same symbolism of fecundity.
Numerology: the triangle of three has now become a square, either because it has a fourth side, or because by manifesting on earth, heaven has reflected itself and so the mirrored Kabbalah diagram begins to appear, thus:

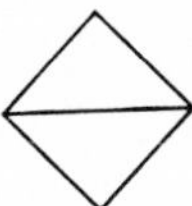

Four is also the number of matter, i.e. the four elements.*

Glyph: 4, which is half a square (incomplete) together with the cross of matter; or the figure of Man trapped within matter, but reaching upwards towards heaven.

Thirteen is the first compound number of four.
Tarot: 'the Reaper', which stands for rejuvenation; the death of the old and birth of the new.
Numerology: the number of upheavals and destruction, of removing decay in order to clear the way for new beginnings. It can bring change of plans, place and so on. It is not unlucky as is generally supposed, for it is associated with death only in the sense of the dying away of the unwanted past.

Twenty-two is not in the tortoise diagram, but is included here as it is associated with the Tarot trump Zero.
Tarot: the last of the Tarot trumps is twenty-one, but, in the Tarot, twenty-two is associated with Zero (as just mentioned) because both have the same type of powerful force. As mentioned below under 'Numerology', twenty-two is a master number. Zero and twenty-two both represent a potent power

* These four elements, namely earth, air, fire and water, should not be confused with the Five States of Change of the *I Ching*, which are sometimes erroneously referred to as 'elements'.

which causes things to move and both are thus associated with the raising of kundalini.

In the mundane sense this number, Zero, represents 'the Fool', which depicts a good man blinded by the stupidity of other people, living in a fool's paradise. It therefore carries warning of illusion and delusion.
Numerology: this is similar to the number eleven, but because this is doubled, it contains twice the 'master' power, being a higher octave of eleven; thus standing for idealism of a deeper and also more practical kind.

Five (The number of change)
I Ching: the Wind ☴, the indecisive and also the decisive. This trigram represents the air or physical breath, the vitalizing breath of spirit, the renewal of life and thus the link between spirit and body, heaven and earth, yang and yin.
Tortoise: the central position; that is, the place where yang and yin meet, and where the cosmic forces interact.
Kabbalah: Geburah, severity.
Commandment: 'Honour thy father and thy mother.' This refers to the yang and yin force, and to honour this is to acknowledge the fact that humanity is not mere animal, but a child of the Divine father/mother who must be obeyed and with whom Man must co-operate.
Tarot: 'the Hierophant, Pope or High Priest', which refers to the temple of the Divine, which is the mind. Also for the dispensing of welfare and everything which is needed for the well-being of existence.
Numerology: the mind, freedom, movement, travel, not necessarily physical motion, but referring perhaps more often to mental expansion such as study; or to spiritual movement, as the result of religious experiences.
Glyph: **5** symbolizing the union of the half square of earth (yin) with the incomplete circle of heaven (yang).

Fourteen is the first compound number of five.

Tarot: 'Temperance'. Whilst the number five represents 'the Hierophant', who is the leader of a religious sect, or, as has already been pointed out, can represent the mind, the number fourteen symbolizes the building in which the religion is conducted, in other words, the physical brain.
Numerology: union and its opposite, disunion or unfortunate combinations. In the *I Ching* these opposing influences are those which cause the switching of yang and yin, back and forth, pulling away, then coming together again.

Six

I Ching and Tortoise: Water ☵, the Abysmal, darkness, danger; of being true to oneself; of keeping to the path of duty. It symbolizes spirit trapped within the physical. The unconscious, unaware, unknowing, instinctive.
Kabbalah: Tiphereth, beauty.
Commandment: 'Thou shalt not kill.' This means that any attempt made to express the right way of living must never be stamped out.
Tarot: 'the Lovers', which stands for the purity and innocence of human love. As with the meeting of Adam and Eve in the garden of Eden in simplicity, that is, without having tasted of the fruit of the tree of knowledge, so also it depicts the fall of Man and his choice between the path of good or evil.
Numerology: the home, love. It signifies two paths from which Man must choose either the upward climb of duty, aspiring to the good and positive, pictured by the male lover (yang); or the downward negative easy path of pleasure depicted by the female lover (yin).

There are many symbols connected with this number, perhaps the best-known being the two interlaced triangles of the Star of David (or Seal of Solomon), the number of whose lines is six, the two triangles depicting the trinities of God and Man intertwined or reflected as in the Kabbalah diagram.

There is also the black and white *I Ching* symbol of the intertwined positive and negative forces, sometimes called *soixante-neuf*, six being an inverted nine, symbolizing 'the Lovers' in the Tarot in a sexual posture, thus:

The trigram of Water, as the symbol of emotions and desires, also represents the moon of lovers. It is the great divider in occultism; for example, the River Styx which is said to separate heaven and earth; Christian baptism which uses water to symbolize the cleansing from evil; and a surgeon who 'scrubs up' so that his patient may be protected from germs, sickness (evil).

There is also the six-portioned cross formed from the unfolded cube, or the square of earth, thus:

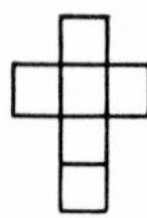

forming the cross of love which symbolizes the choice of the upward path. The closed cube of the negative earth becomes opened out and transformed as Man learns to crucify, or kill out the lower desires, learns to avoid the downward path and develop the aspiring higher aspect of himself. This number, therefore, represents the love principle struggling in matter towards the light.

Glyph: 6 in which the complete circle of earth reaches upward to heavenly existence.

Fifteen is the first compound number of six.

Tarot: 'the Devil', representing lust and showing a person who could easily become blinded to the path of service to others. It also symbolizes Adam and Eve after they have been driven out of the garden of Eden.

Numerology: a very potent number, being considered the number of occultism and magic. In River Lo the numbers add up to fifteen whether they be read horizontally, vertically or diagonally which is a well-known Chinese puzzle, thus:

4	9	2
3	5	7
8	1	6

Seven

I Ching and Tortoise: the Mountain ☶, Stillness; also meditation, prayer, stilling the mind as well as the body; communing with God. It also symbolizes a barrier or gateway for it represents the end of life.
Kabbalah: Netzach, victory.
Commandment: 'Thou shalt not commit adultery.' Seven is the number of perfection, and that which is perfect must be pure without contamination (adulteration).
Tarot: 'the Chariot', which shows a victorious figure riding in a chariot; one who has overcome many of the trials of life and has now liberated himself.
Numerology: this is the perfect number, there being seven colours, notes of music, days of the week; seven Spirits before the Throne of God. It is the number of mysticism, being a point of contact between the lower and higher Self or the conscious and the unconscious at a time of sleep or meditation. The number is made up of four and three, referring to the triplicities and quadruplicities of astrology, or that the four (of matter) has become joined to the three (of heaven).

Glyph: 7 which is 4 inverted, so to speak, that is matter (four) transformed.

Sixteen is the first compound number of seven.
Tarot: 'the Struck Tower', which represents the law of cause and effect or Karma. In this sense this number ties up with the idea of the gateway to heaven of the *I Ching* Mountain symbol. Man has to strive to build his Tower, which must be perfect or it will collapse and probably bury him underneath

the ruins, and if this should happen, he will have to crawl out from underneath and begin to rebuild his life anew.
Numerology: symbolizes reincarnation, the cycle of life, death and rebirth. Sixteen can be a warning of adverse action by Fate, against which, wherever possible, provision should be made.

Eight

I Ching and the Tortoise: the Receptive ☷, the yin principle, opposition, Man's earthly nature. The two circles or figure-of-eight of this number symbolize heaven and earth or the cosmic switching of yang and yin. There are eight trigrams because there are eight digits when the number five (of change) *or* nine (of non-change) are omitted (see also the other number of earth, or yin, which is two).
Kabbalah: Hod, splendour.
Commandment: 'Thou shalt not steal.' The lower Self must not be allowed to steal from the higher. The Great Law will imprison Man on earth until he has learned not to steal from heaven and misuse celestial gifts.
Tarot: 'Justice', which stands for righteousness and the triumph of good over evil, and for weighing things in the balance, the two circles of the figure eight depicting the higher and lower life.
Numerology: balance and the number of matter (four) doubled (twice four), justice and inspiration.

Glyph: **8**. Two circles one above the other which intercommunicate symbolizing that Man is in touch with heaven, has achieved a state of balance between the pairs of opposites and reached a certain stage of completion (because it is a circle), ready to move on to the next number, nine, which is initiation.

Seventeen is the first compound number of eight.
Tarot: 'the Star of Attainment', 'the eight-pointed Star of

the Magi' or the Masons' 'l'étoile flamboyante' referred to earlier in this work. It represents attainment to a state where the waters of life are freely given and freely absorbed; where the gifts of the spirit are received.
Numerology: immortality, and, in a physical sense, fame.

Nine

I Ching: there is no trigram associated with this number, there being only eight trigrams, because the trigrams are symbolic of states of change and the number nine is incapable of change. It is the number of heaven (or pre-heaven).
Tortoise: at the head, which indicates not only the ability to achieve, but also to communicate.
Kabbalah: Yesod, foundation.
Commandment: 'Thou shalt not bear false witness against thy neighbour.' 'Thy neighbour' is anyone who may be encountered, including yourself. Only when Man can face himself in truth and see himself as he really is, and know the true motives of his actions, can he be ready for the great initiation of this number, into the mysteries. 'Man, know thyself' was engraved upon the shrine of the Delphic Oracle, and this is what it means.
Tarot: 'the Hermit', which stands for maturity and experience, i.e. a person who guides and helps others by his spiritual light. Such wisdom, virtue or light is obtained by having passed through all the tests of life, and having risen above them, triumphant.
Numerology: impersonal love, understanding and service to humanity, faith, a teacher, true prophet, seer and miracle-worker.

Glyph: **9** which is the opposite of the number six, where there was a choice between two paths. Having been inverted, the circle of earth reaching upwards has now become the circle of heaven reaching downwards to help and comfort humanity.

Eighteen is the first compound number of nine.
Tarot: 'the Waning Moon' which stands for the final gateway into the unknown.
Numerology: can be taken to symbolize the negative aspect of materialism striving to destroy the spiritual side of nature. Thus, even at the very moment of initiation when Man is ready for the next step, that is the ten of completion, he is still open to the influence of yin as well as yang.

It is only when he enters the very centre of the circle where T'ai Chi dwells that he can be free of the constant tug-of-war between yang and yin; then, and only then, will he find union with all—*and* the peace that passeth all understanding, liberation, Nirvana, because he will then have reached perfection, and become as the Absolute Utmost, T'ai Chi. In such a state he must of necessity, according to the *I Ching*, manifest creatively upon the earth in some form, and thus become part of the endless process of enantiodromia, which is eternally being played out in creation.

Diagrams

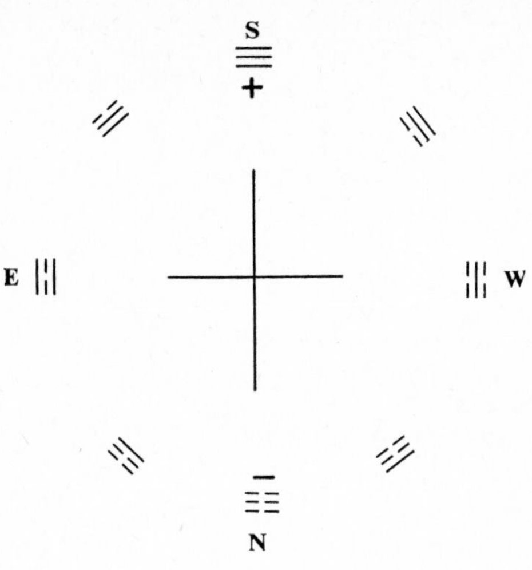

1 Pre-heaven

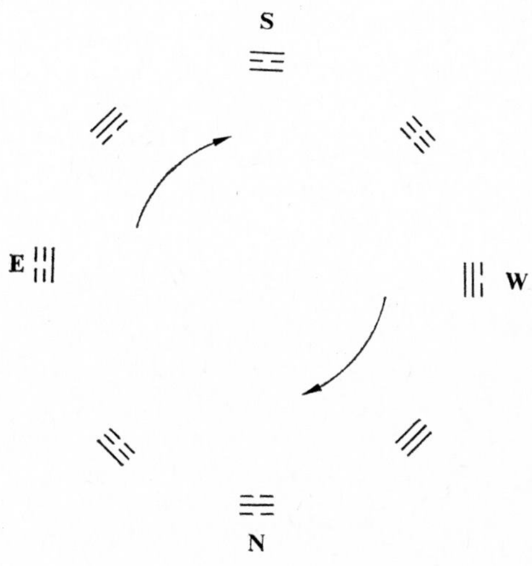

2 Later-heaven

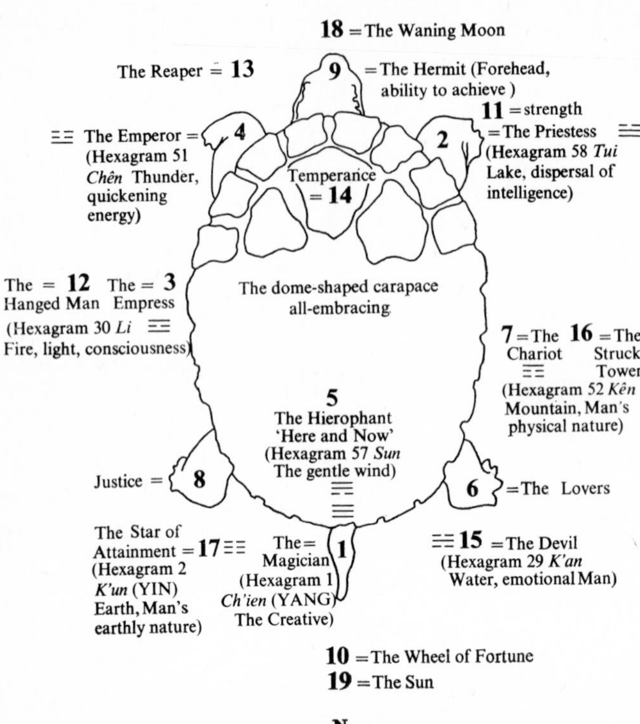

3 The Chinese tortoise

(*Note:* The heavy numbers represent the Tarot delineation. The symbols and smaller numbers are taken from the *I Ching*.)

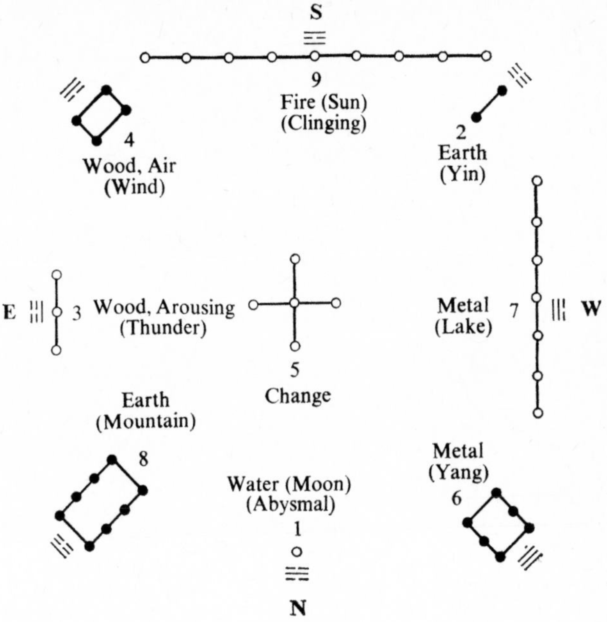

S

9
Fire (Sun)
(Clinging)

4
Wood, Air
(Wind)

2
Earth
(Yin)

E 3 Wood, Arousing
(Thunder)

5
Change

Metal
(Lake) 7 W

Earth
(Mountain)
8

Water (Moon)
(Abysmal)
1

Metal
(Yang)
6

N

4 The Writing from the River Lo Map (tortoise)

5 The dragon-horse of the *I Ching*

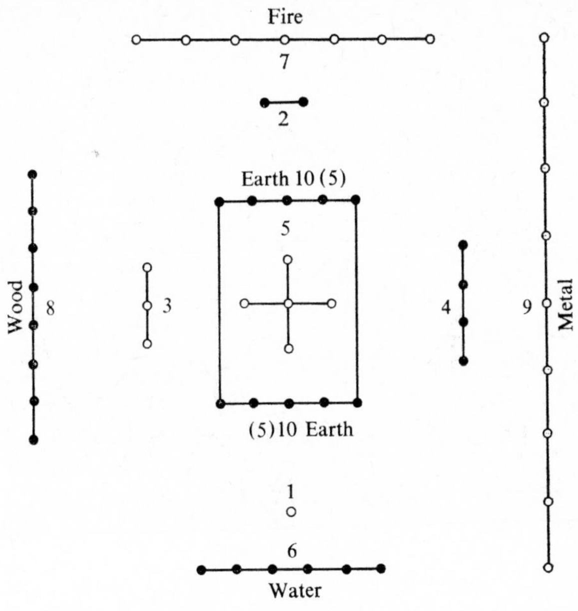

6 The Yellow River Map (dragon-horse)

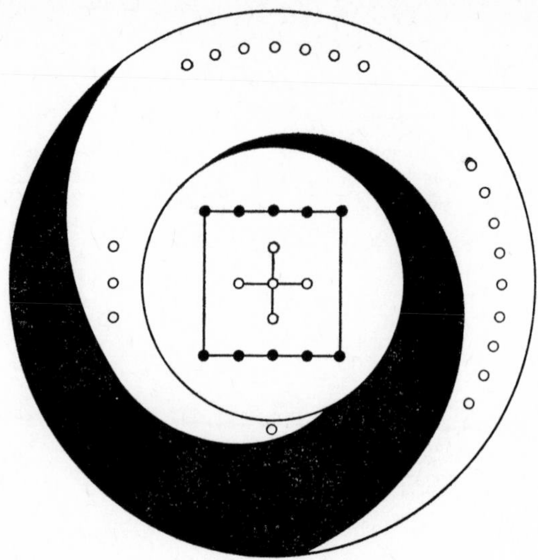

7 The development of the pattern of the *I Ching* from the Yellow River Map

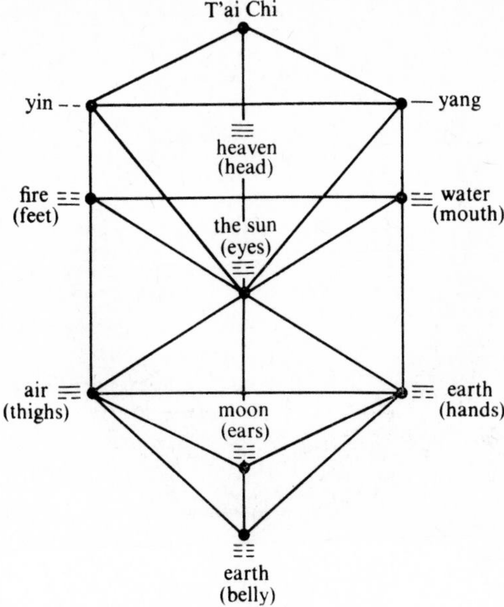

8 The Chinese cosmos

(*Note:* This is a diagram of the human frame shown facing you, i.e. its left side is shown on the right.)

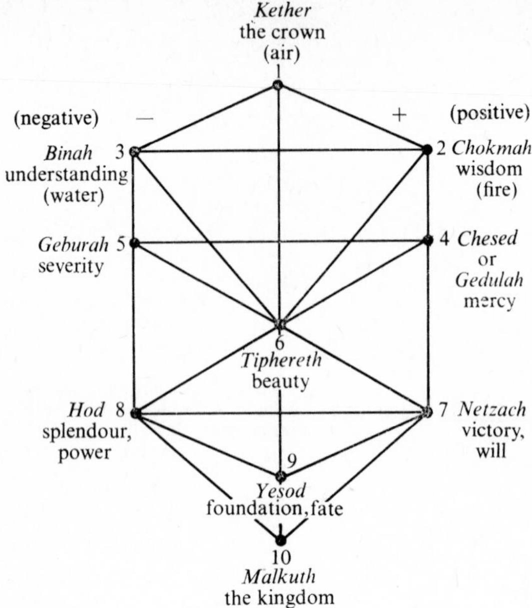

9 The Sephirothal tree of life of the Kabbalah

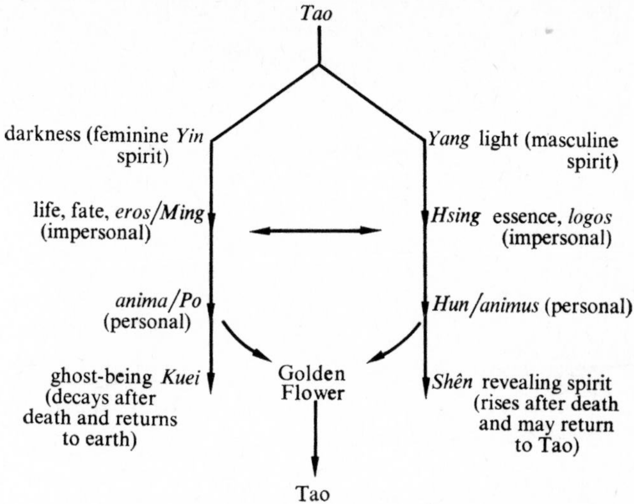

10 Chinese concepts concerned with the development of the Golden Flower or immortal Spirit Body

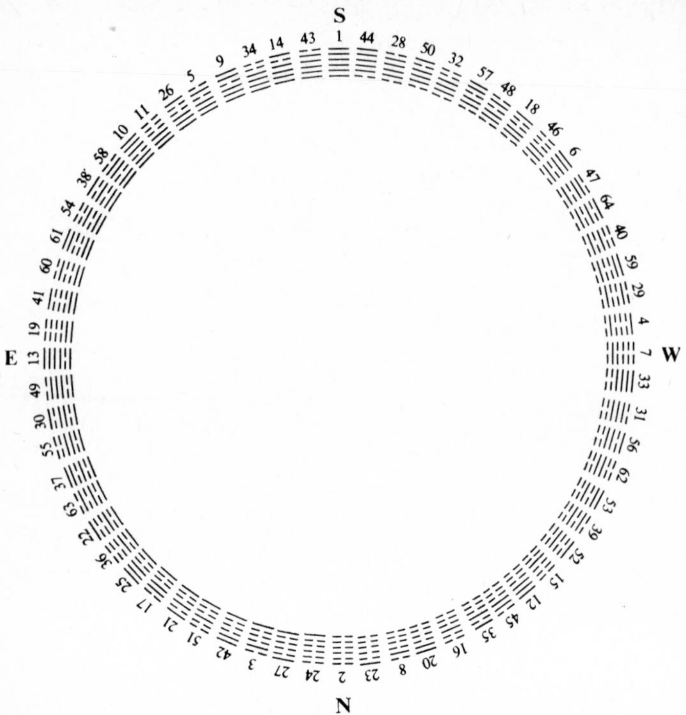

11 Shao Yung's sequence of the hexagrams

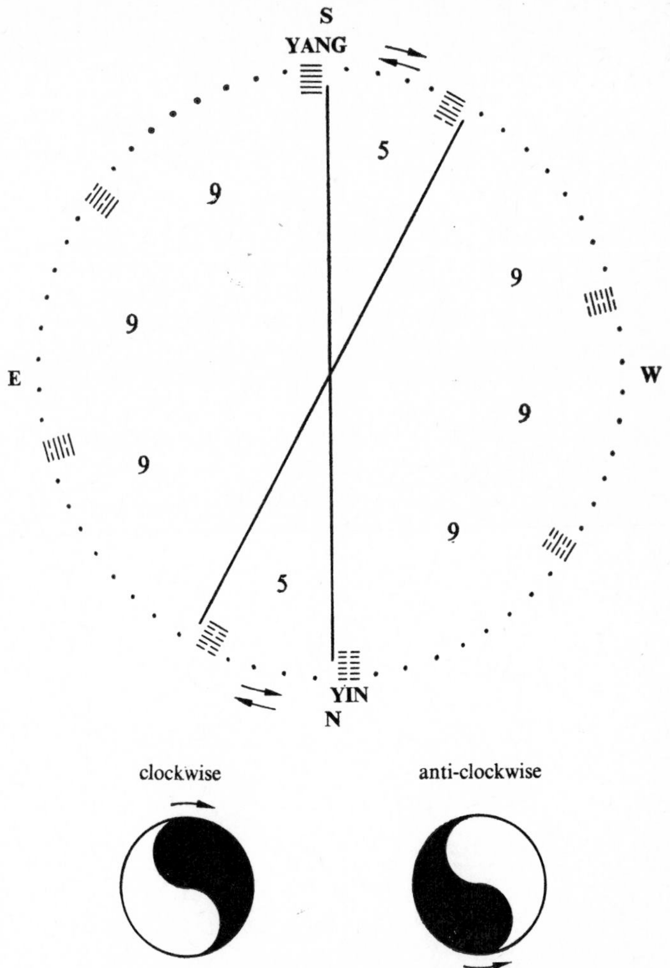

12 Shao Yung's sequence showing the reciprocal action of yang and yin upon each other and the other hexagrams (indicated by dots unless doubled trigrams)

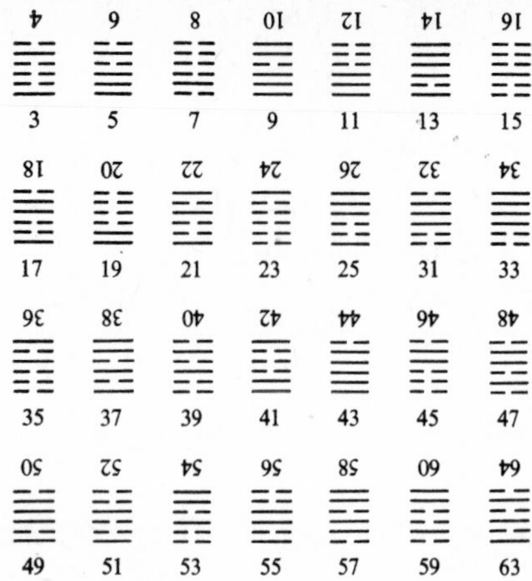

(a) Table of reversible ideograms

(b) Table of non-reversible ideograms

13 The numerical sequence of all the hexagrams of the *I Ching* shown in pairs

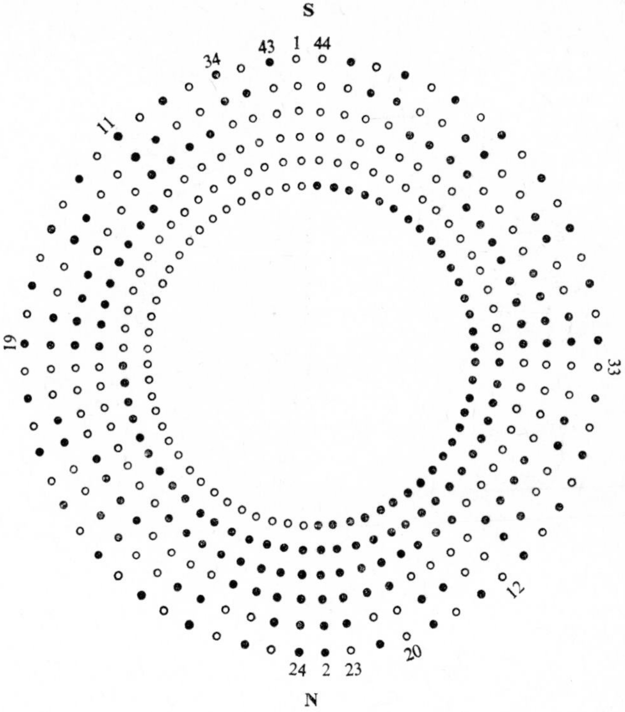

14 Shao Yung's sequence

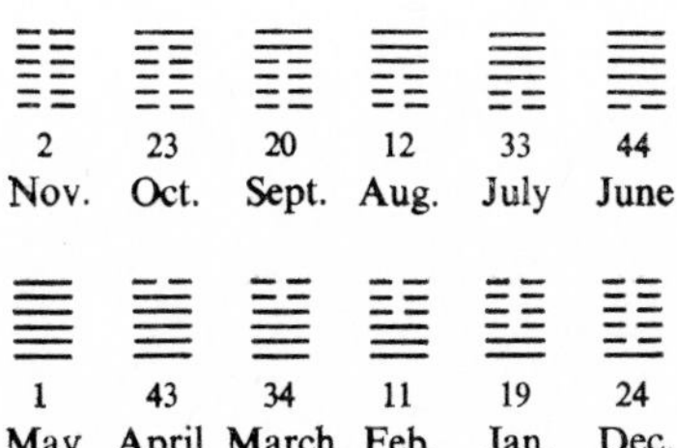

15 The calendar hexagrams

(*Note:* The months have been shown in this order so that the hexagram line build-up coincides with Shao Yung's sequence.)

16 Shao Yung's sequence showing the divisions of yang and yin (where like attracts like leading to the attraction of opposites)

(*Notes:* 1. The outer trigrams only are divided by small lines; 2. The yang force is present as a thin white dividing line within the yin (running south/north).)

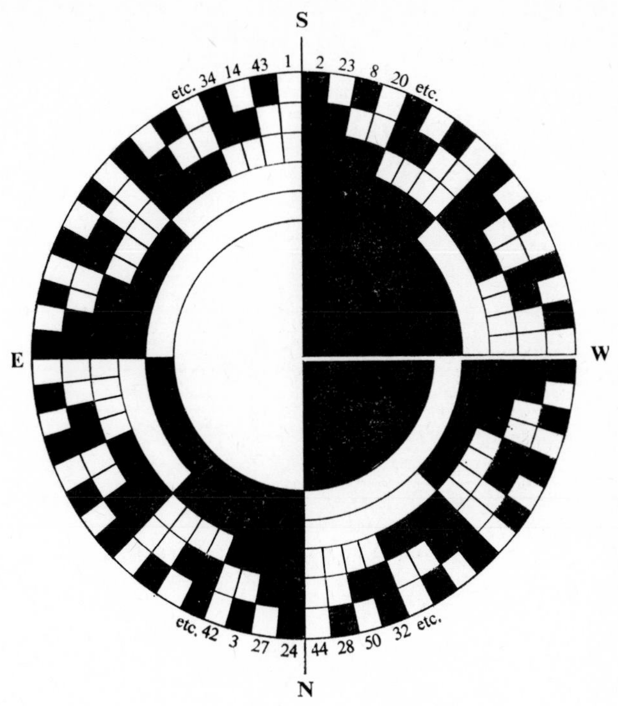

17 Shao Yung's sequence reversed at south and north (where there is the attraction of opposites leading to like attracting like)

(*Notes:* 1. The outer trigrams only are divided by small lines; 2. The yang force is present as a thin white dividing line within the yin (running east/west).)

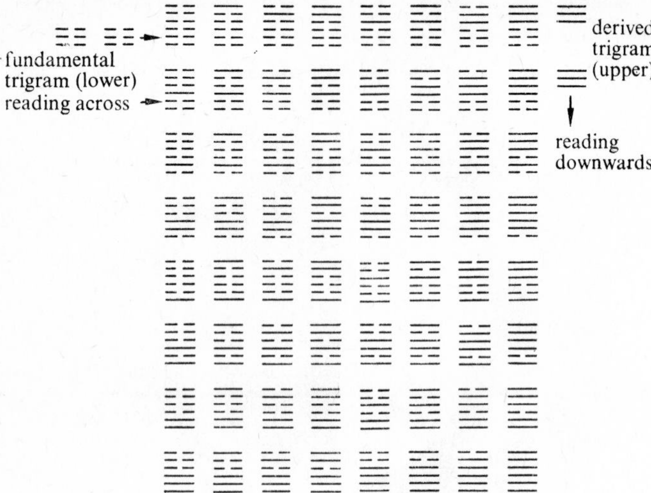

18 Shao Yung's square sequence

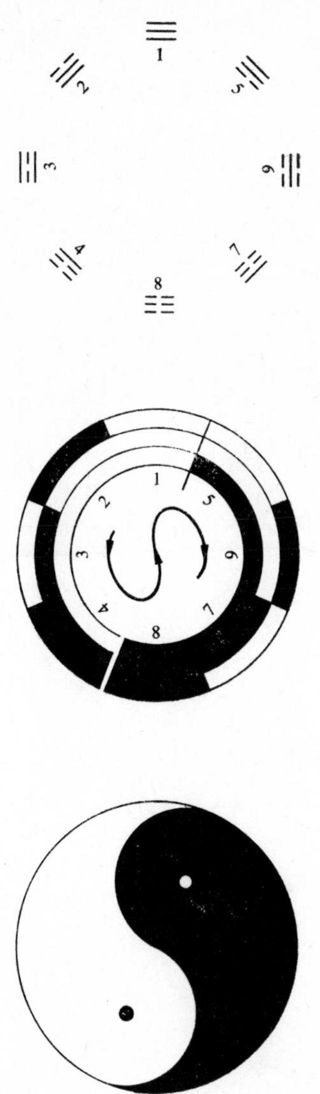

19 The switching of yang and yin in pre-heaven

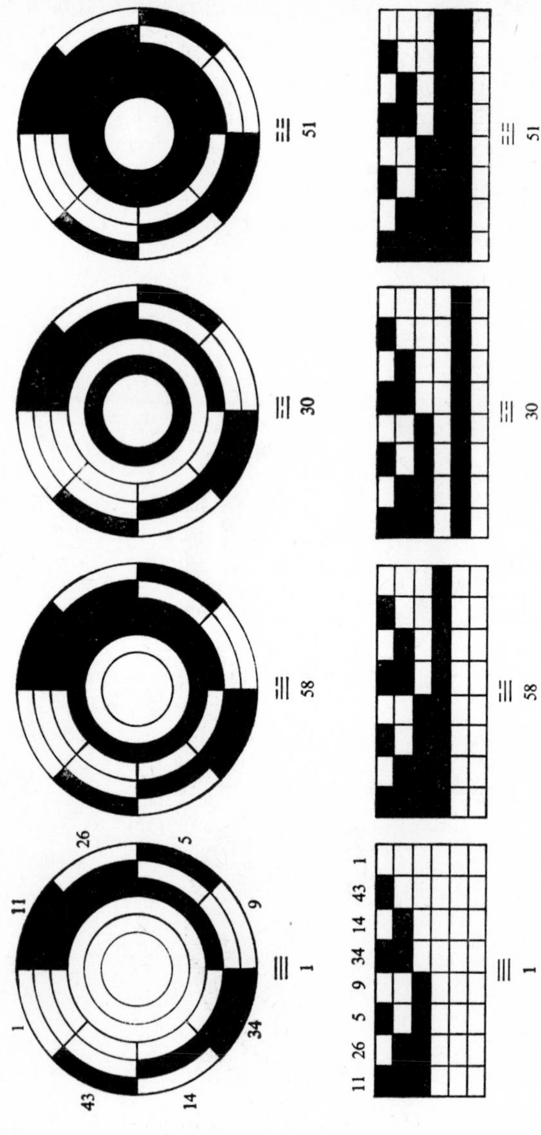

20 The inside and outside trigrams comprising the hexagrams of Shao Yung's circular and square diagrams

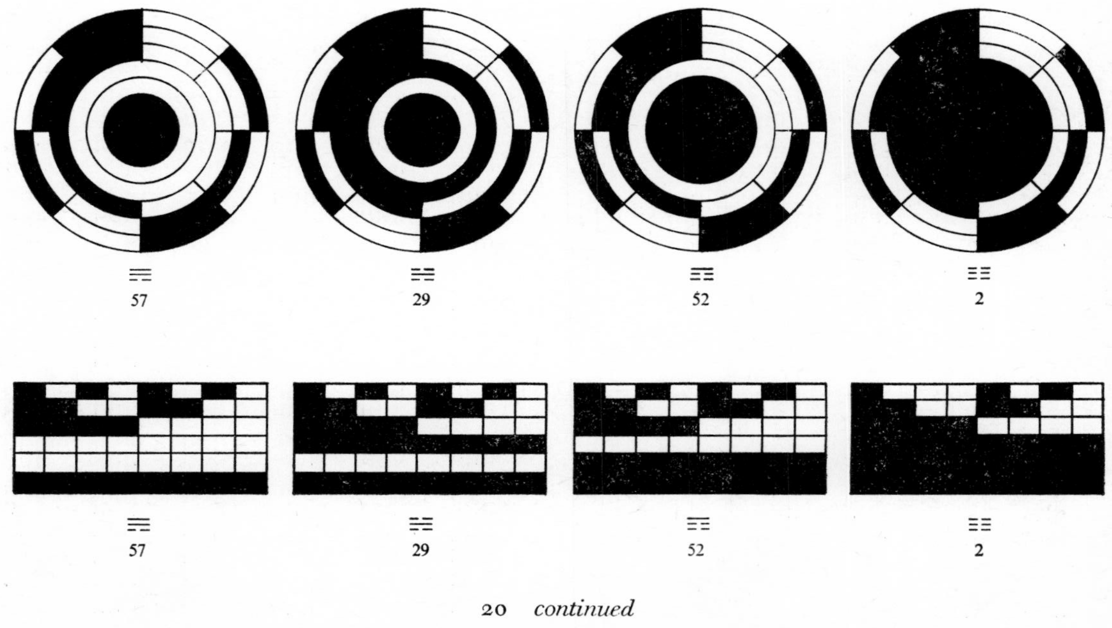

20 *continued*

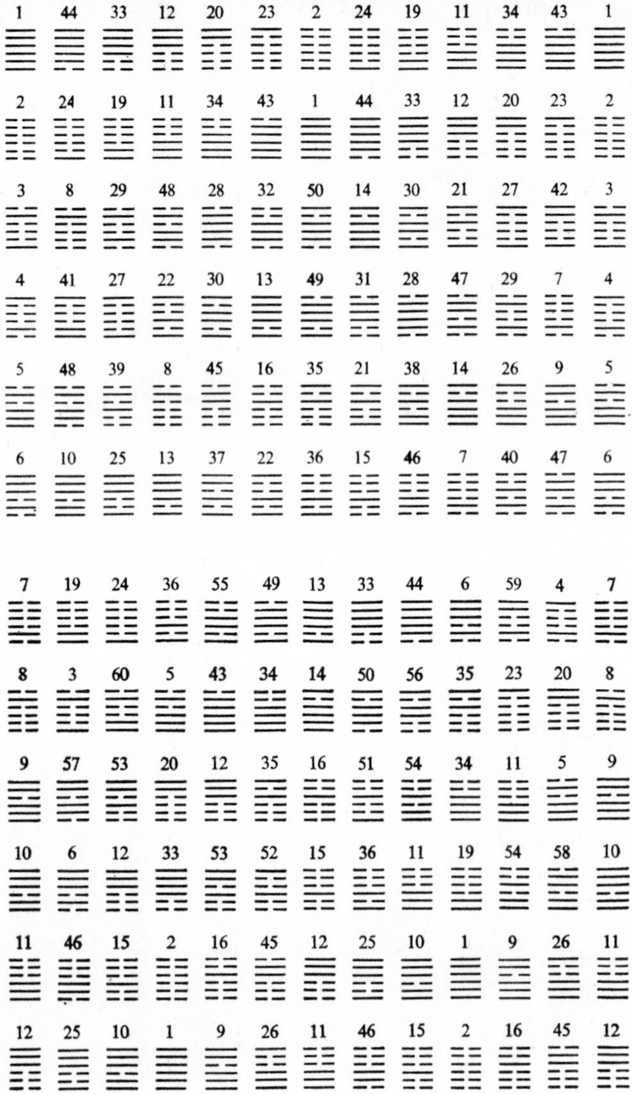

1 44 33 12 20 23 2 24 19 11 34 43 1

2 24 19 11 34 43 1 44 33 12 20 23 2

3 8 29 48 28 32 50 14 30 21 27 42 3

4 41 27 22 30 13 49 31 28 47 29 7 4

5 48 39 8 45 16 35 21 38 14 26 9 5

6 10 25 13 37 22 36 15 46 7 40 47 6

7 19 24 36 55 49 13 33 44 6 59 4 7

8 3 60 5 43 34 14 50 56 35 23 20 8

9 57 53 20 12 35 16 51 54 34 11 5 9

10 6 12 33 53 52 15 36 11 19 54 58 10

11 46 15 2 16 45 12 25 10 1 9 26 11

12 25 10 1 9 26 11 46 15 2 16 45 12

21 Mutating hexagrams

13 33 44 6 59 4 7 19 24 36 55 49 13

14 50 56 35 23 20 8 3 60 5 43 34 14

15 36 11 19 54 58 10 6 12 33 53 52 15

16 51 54 34 11 5 9 57 53 20 12 35 16

17 45 47 28 48 46 18 26 22 27 21 25 17

18 26 22 27 21 25 17 45 47 28 48 46 18

19 7 2 15 62 31 33 13 1 10 61 41 19

20 42 61 9 1 14 34 32 62 16 2 8 20

21 35 64 50 18 57 48 5 63 3 17 51 21

22 52 18 4 64 6 47 58 17 49 63 36 22

23 27 41 26 14 1 43 28 31 45 8 2 23

24 2 7 46 32 28 44 1 13 25 42 27 24

21 *continued*

25 12 6 44 57 18 46 11 36 24 51 17 25

26 18 52 23 35 12 45 17 58 43 5 11 26

27 23 4 18 50 44 28 43 49 17 3 24 27

28 43 49 17 3 24 27 23 4 18 50 44 28

29 60 3 63 49 55 30 56 50 64 4 59 29

30 56 50 64 4 59 29 60 3 63 49 55 30

31 49 43 58 60 19 41 4 23 52 56 33 31

32 34 55 51 24 3 42 20 59 57 44 50 32

33 13 1 10 61 41 19 7 2 15 62 31 33

34 32 62 16 2 8 20 42 61 9 1 14 34

35 21 38 14 26 9 5 48 39 8 45 16 35

36 15 46 7 40 47 6 10 25 13 37 22 36

21 *continued*

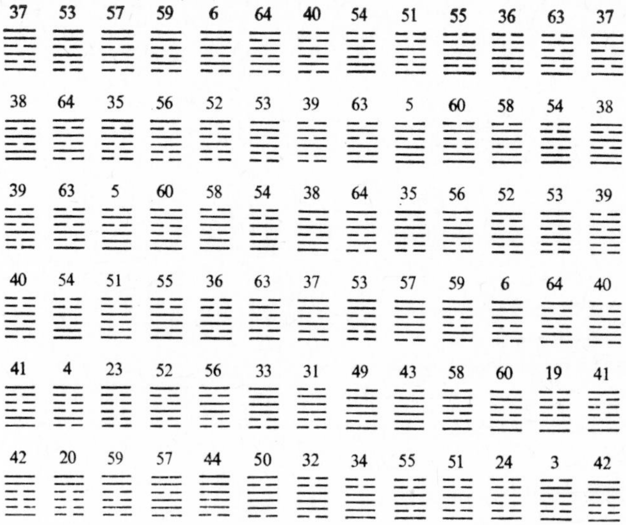

37	53	57	59	6	64	40	54	51	55	36	63	37
38	64	35	56	52	53	39	63	5	60	58	54	38
39	63	5	60	58	54	38	64	35	56	52	53	39
40	54	51	55	36	63	37	53	57	59	6	64	40
41	4	23	52	56	33	31	49	43	58	60	19	41
42	20	59	57	44	50	32	34	55	51	24	3	42

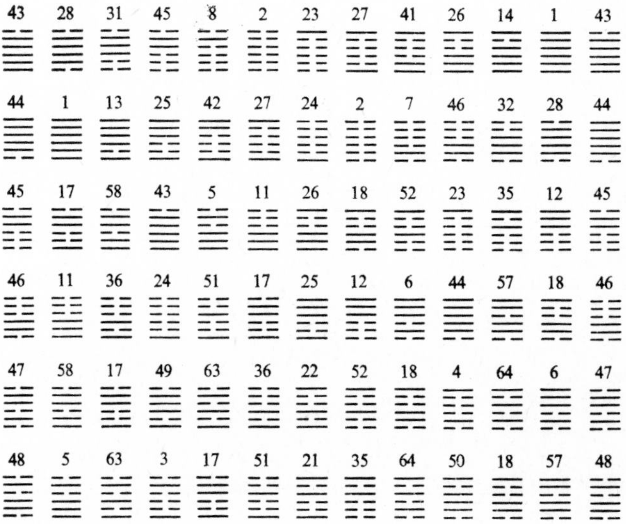

43	28	31	45	8	2	23	27	41	26	14	1	43
44	1	13	25	42	27	24	2	7	46	32	28	44
45	17	58	43	5	11	26	18	52	23	35	12	45
46	11	36	24	51	17	25	12	6	44	57	18	46
47	58	17	49	63	36	22	52	18	4	64	6	47
48	5	63	3	17	51	21	35	64	50	18	57	48

21 *continued*

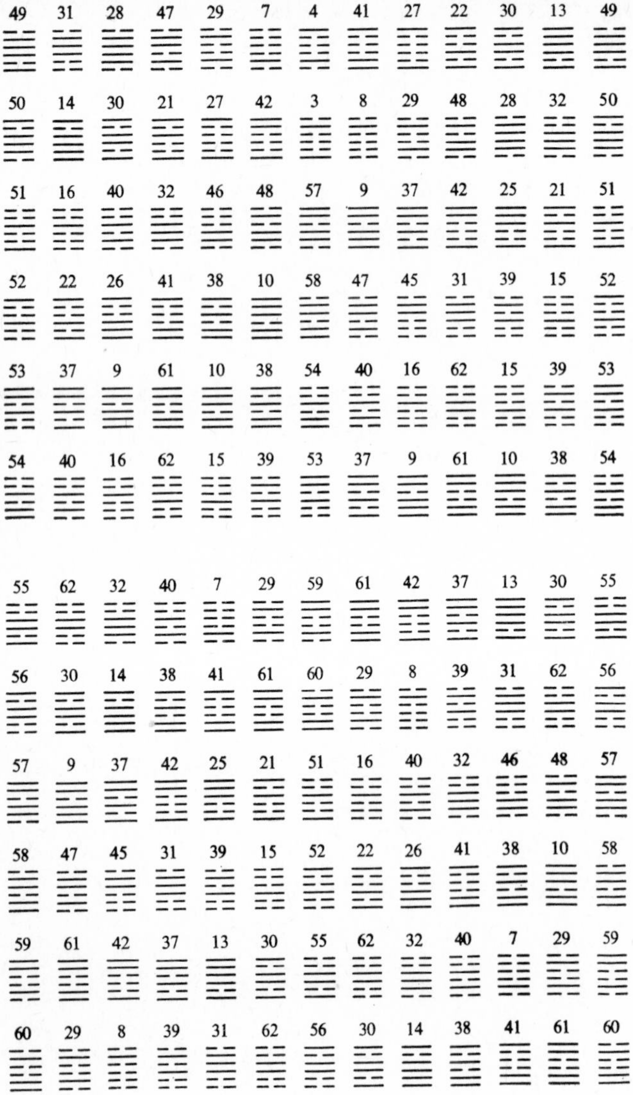

49 31 28 47 29 7 4 41 27 22 30 13 49

50 14 30 21 27 42 3 8 29 48 28 32 50

51 16 40 32 46 48 57 9 37 42 25 21 51

52 22 26 41 38 10 58 47 45 31 39 15 52

53 37 9 61 10 38 54 40 16 62 15 39 53

54 40 16 62 15 39 53 37 9 61 10 38 54

55 62 32 40 7 29 59 61 42 37 13 30 55

56 30 14 38 41 61 60 29 8 39 31 62 56

57 9 37 42 25 21 51 16 40 32 46 48 57

58 47 45 31 39 15 52 22 26 41 38 10 58

59 61 42 37 13 30 55 62 32 40 7 29 59

60 29 8 39 31 62 56 30 14 38 41 61 60

21 *continued*

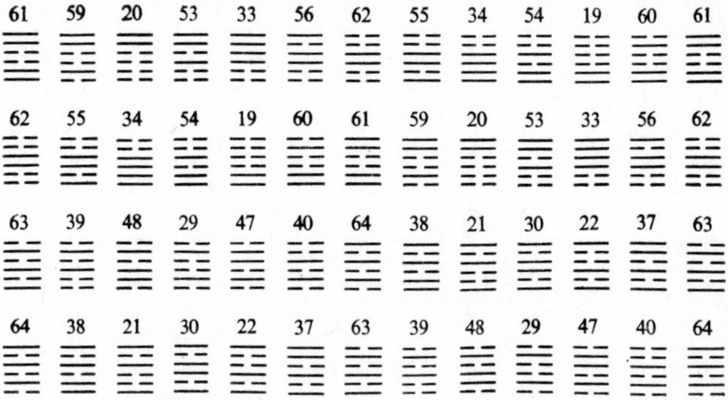

61	59	20	53	33	56	62	55	34	54	19	60	61
62	55	34	54	19	60	61	59	20	53	33	56	62
63	39	48	29	47	40	64	38	21	30	22	37	63
64	38	21	30	22	37	63	39	48	29	47	40	64

21 *continued*

(*Note:* The above are applicable when the cycles are repetitive such as days, weeks, seasons, years, etc.)

1 Creative	2 Abysmal	3 Keeping Still	4 Arousing	5 Gentle	6 Clinging	7 Receptive	8 Joyous
1	29	52	51	57	30	2	58
44	60	22	16	9	56	24	47
33	3	26	40	37	50	19	45
12	63	41	32	42	64	11	31
20	49	38	46	25	4	34	39
23	55	10	48	21	59	43	15
35	36	61	28	27	6	5	62
14	7	53	17	18	13	8	54

22 The houses of the *I Ching*

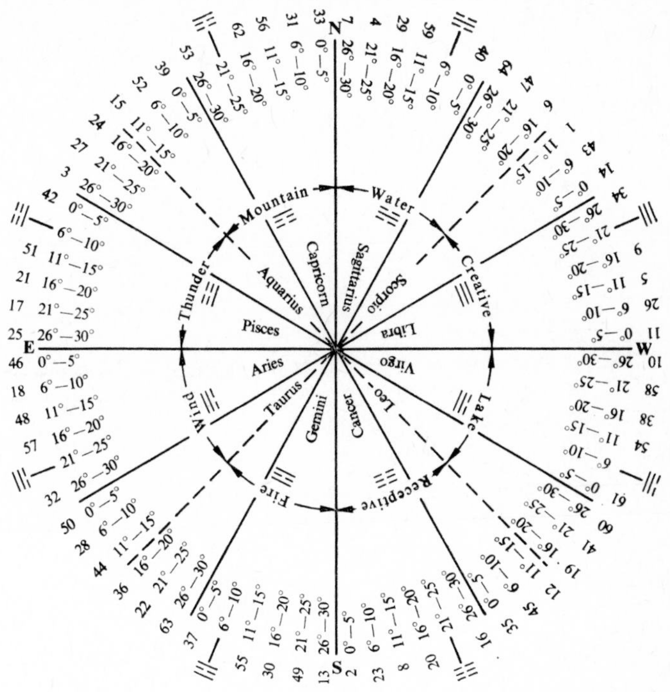

23 Chart showing the trigrams of the *I Ching* and the signs of the Zodiac to which they refer, in the order normal to astrologers

(*Note:* The hexagram numbers appear on the perimeter.)

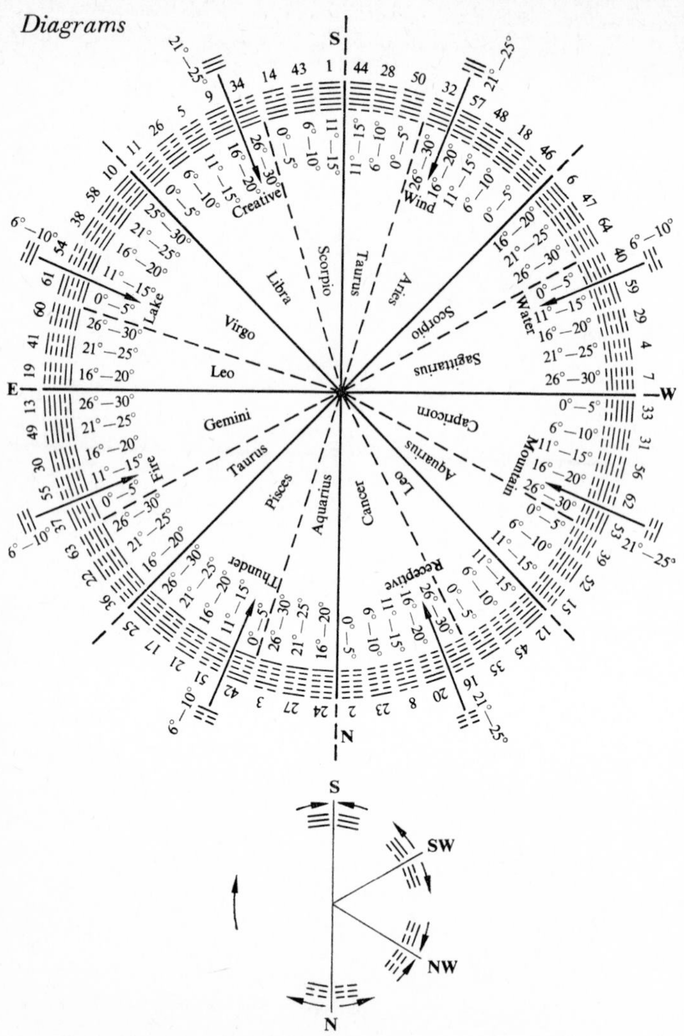

24 Shao Yung's sequence of the hexagrams of the *I Ching* (in the pre-heaven arrangement of the trigrams) and the signs and degrees of the Zodiac

(*Note:* The arrows in this small diagram indicate the reversals of the (normal) progression through the signs and degrees of the Zodiac in Shao Yung's sequence of the hexagrams.)

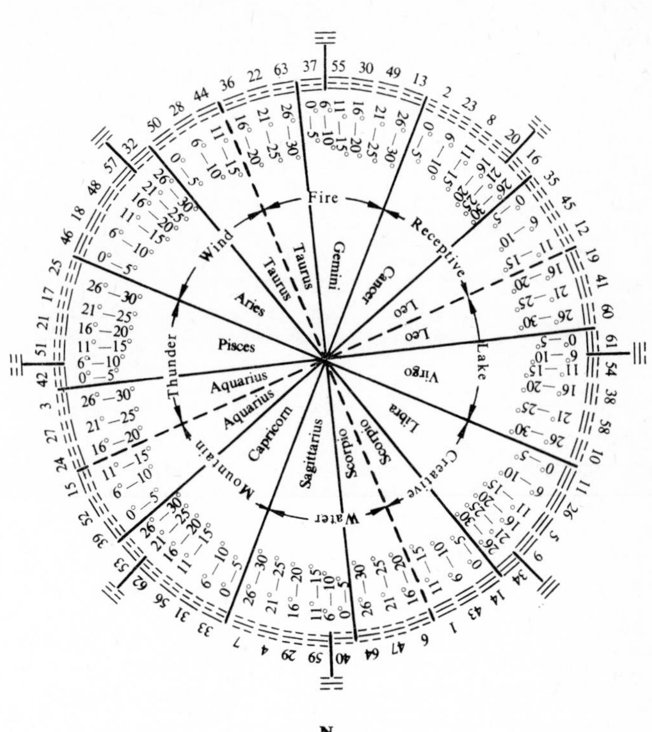

25 The signs of the Zodiac based on the later-heaven arrangement of the trigrams

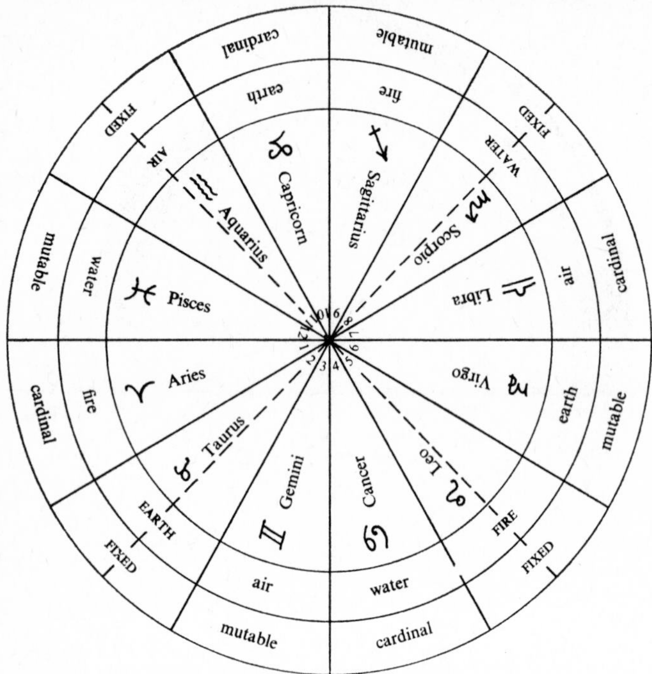

26 The signs of the Zodiac and their symbols and houses, together with the triplicities (elements) and quadruplicities (natures)*

* See table on p. 96.

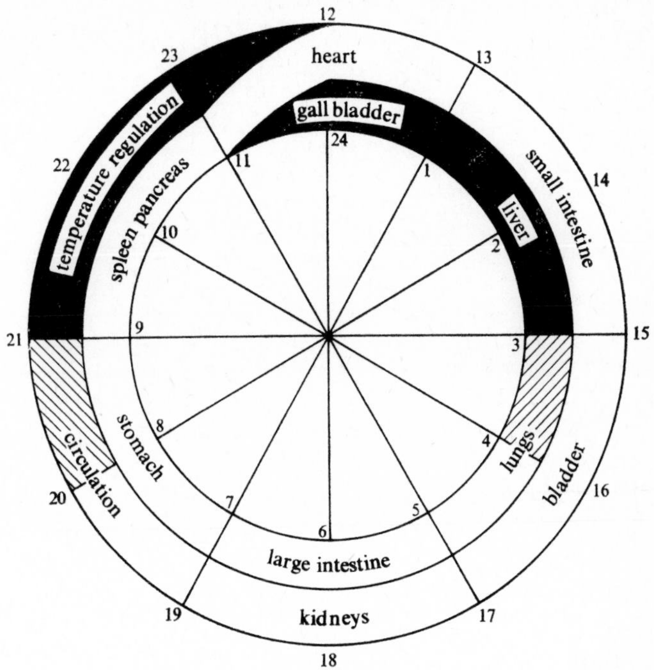

27 The Chinese organ clock
(twenty-four-hour)

Bibliography

Albertson, Edward (1969), *The Complete I Ching for the Millions*, Sherbourne Press, Los Angeles.

Blofeld, John (trs.) (1965), *The Book of Change*, Allen & Unwin; paperback edn, E. P. Dutton, New York.

Boyle, Veolita Parke (1934), *The Fundamental Principles of the Yi-King Tao*, W. & G. Foyle.

Cheiro, Louis Hamon (1935), *Cheiro's Book of Numbers*, H. Jenkins.

Curtiss, F. Homer (1938), *The Key to the Universe*, Curtiss Philosophic Book Co., Washington.

Douglas, Alfred (1971), *The Oracle of Change*, Gollancz.

'Edited I Ching Diagrams and Explanations' (untranslated from Chinese), The Great New Book Co., Taipei, Taiwan.

Foote, Mary (1963), *The Interpretation of Visions IV* (Notes on a Seminar by C. G. Jung), *Spring*, 1963, Spring Publications, Zurich.

Hone, M. E. (1951), *The Modern Textbook of Astrology*, L. N. Fowler.

Hook, Diana ffarington (1973), *The I Ching and You*, Routledge & Kegan Paul; paperback edn, E. P. Dutton, New York.

Jung, C. G. (1963), *Memories, Dreams and Reflections*, Routledge & Kegan Paul.

Jung, C. G. (1964), *Man and His Symbols*, Aldus Books in association with W. H. Allen.

Krishnamurti, J. (1910), *At the Feet of the Master*, The Theosophical Publishing House.

Legge, James (trs.) (1963), *I Ching: The Book of Changes*, The Sacred Books of the East, vol. 16, Dover Publications, New York.

Leo, Alan (1967), *Esoteric Astrology*, L. N. Fowler.

Leo, Alan (1970) *Jupiter: The Preserver*, Samuel Weiser, New York.

Mayo, Jeff (1964), *Teach Yourself Astrology*, English Universities Press.

Mears, I. and Mears, L. E. (1931), *Creative Energy*, John Murray (out of print).

Peters, J. F. (n.d.), *Mis-mated*, Staples Press.

Sanders, C. G. (1925), *Practical Numerology*, C. W. Daniel (out of print).

Sherrill, W. A. (1972), *Heritage of Change*, East-West Eclectic Society, Taipei, Taiwan.

Stiefvater, E. W. (1955), *What is Acupuncture?* (trs. by L. O. Korth), Health Science Press.

Velikovsky, I. (1950), *Worlds in Collision*, Gollancz.

Waite, A. E. (n.d.), *The Key to the Tarot*, Rider & Co.

Wilhelm, Hellmut (1961), *Change: Eight Lectures on the I Ching* (trs. by Cary F. Baynes), Routledge & Kegan Paul.

Wilhelm, R. and Jung, C. G. (1931), *The Secret of the Golden Flower: A Chinese Book of Life* (trs. by Cary F. Baynes), Routledge & Kegan Paul and Harcourt Brace Jovanovich, New York.

Wilhelm, R. (trs.) (1951), *The I Ching or Book of Changes* (trs. by Cary F. Baynes), Routledge & Kegan Paul and Princeton University Press, New Jersey.

Willoughby-Meade, G. (1928), *The Sacred Classic of Permutations*, *Chinese Ghouls and Goblins*, Constable & Co.

Index

MA